OFF THE
CHARTS

OFF THE CHARTS

TURNING RESULT CHARTS
INTO PROFITABLE SELECTIONS
AT THE TRACK

By
Nick Borg

DRF Press
NEW YORK

Published by
Daily Racing Form Press
100 Broadway, 7th Floor
New York, NY 10005

ISBN: 0-9700147-5-9
Library of Congress Control Number: 2002114413

Cover and jacket designed by Chris Donofry

Text design by Neuwirth and Associates

Printed in the United States of America

Contents

ACKNOWLEDGMENTS

I WOULD LIKE TO thank *Daily Racing Form* for giving me the opportunity to turn my concept of charting races into a published reality. It was a great experience to work with so many talented and gifted people that take pride in their work.

I have always felt that the success I have achieved personally and professionally in my life stems from the advice and wisdom that have been given to me by my family and friends over the years. On many occasions when I find myself in a tough spot, needing a lift, I tend to drift back to these thoughts—and the laughs that were shared with me—and it always seems to help me through. I want you all to know that your kindness has not gone to waste. In fact, it might be more deeply rooted than you will ever realize. I sincerely thank you all and will never forget.

And to those blue eyes I come home to every night: Thanks for surpassing my dreams.

OFF THE
CHARTS

INTRODUCTION

*T*HE IDEA OF studying race charts didn't appeal to me in my earlier years as a handicapper, mainly because I did well at the cashing windows even without them. But years later I came to realize that there was a substantial amount of information being overlooked in my race analysis without examining the result charts.

I realized that without this necessary information I was missing important racing facts and angles that could easily be translated into a crucial edge—an edge in this case being a deeper insight into an actual race. In the mind of a handicapper, this edge should tip the balance of the race on paper, and point to a particular horse's holding the upper hand in at least one critical area.

After this realization I was sold on the concept that in addition to applying all my knowledge and skills as a handicapper, I should add information from the race-result charts to my daily handicapping routine as well.

Within the realm of each chart lies the most comprehensive, insightful racing information published. In fact, *Daily Racing Form*'s result charts are the purest, most factual report in all of Thoroughbred publishing. Their race charts don't contain any ratings or rankings, and above all, they don't offer any opinions based on predetermined conceptions of the outcome of a race. There is no other source, either in print or on-line, that provides such a complete race report.

The DRF race-result charts contain the sharpest, most accurate account of the running of each race as seen through the eyes of experienced professionals reporting the action. And in essence, for a handicapper, the more factual information used while applying one's experience, skills, and knowledge, the higher the chances of finding a truly decisive edge.

Looking back, I realize that another reason I started using charts was that in many instances the past performances, while derived from the same information that makes up a chart, don't have room to capture every piece of chart data. For example, they do not contain all the fractional times needed to create a horse's full pace line. In races at a mile and a sixteenth, the mile fractional time is not given in the past-performance lines. So how do I know exactly how fast a horse finished or even carried his speed to that point of a particular race?

Such information becomes crucial while trying to evaluate just how much talent and ability a horse might posses. And this information is also needed while trying to compare horses' abilities within a given field.

DRF's charts contain every possible fractional call of time in addition to several other important features. There is no other source that provides such a comprehensive report. I know this well because I have worked for *Daily Racing Form* as a quality-assurance editor for 10 years. In this time I have constantly kept the accuracy of result charts as my primary goal.

The bottom line is that no matter how good a handicapper you are and no matter what level you're currently at, using race charts can make every handicapper better. It will lift your game to a much higher level than you're accustomed to and on a much more consistent basis.

The main goal of this book is to discuss the most effective and profitable ways of keeping charts. Within these pages I will examine and evaluate every category and factor where an edge might exist. I will discuss the most informative concepts and theories in relation to charting races while bringing to the surface the most important angles. In return, these concepts, theories, and angles will bring to the forefront a decisive edge within the body of each race chart.

All that is required to succeed in this informative new world is a keen eye, some patience, dedication, and a little bit of imagination.

1

THE TOOLS

*L*ET'S START BY going over what will be needed to chart the races in the correct manner. Obviously we're going to need a reliable source that supplies us with *Daily Racing Form* charts. These days there are several ways of obtaining these.

The first and oldest way is through the pages of the daily publication. Race-result charts are published for most major racetracks, usually on a next-day basis. These charts are compacted into a slightly abbreviated format in order to free up space in the daily newspaper.

The best method of obtaining and saving complete DRF race charts is to subscribe to or purchase *DRF Simulcast Weekly*. This publication, which was created by and for serious players, features a wealth of statistical information including the full race-result charts from the prior week for most major tracks.

Finally, *Daily Racing Form* also offers result charts through its website at www.drf.com.

The following illustration shows a race-result chart taken from the pages of *Daily Racing Form.* I highlighted and labeled each feature of the chart to clarify exactly what constitutes a race chart.

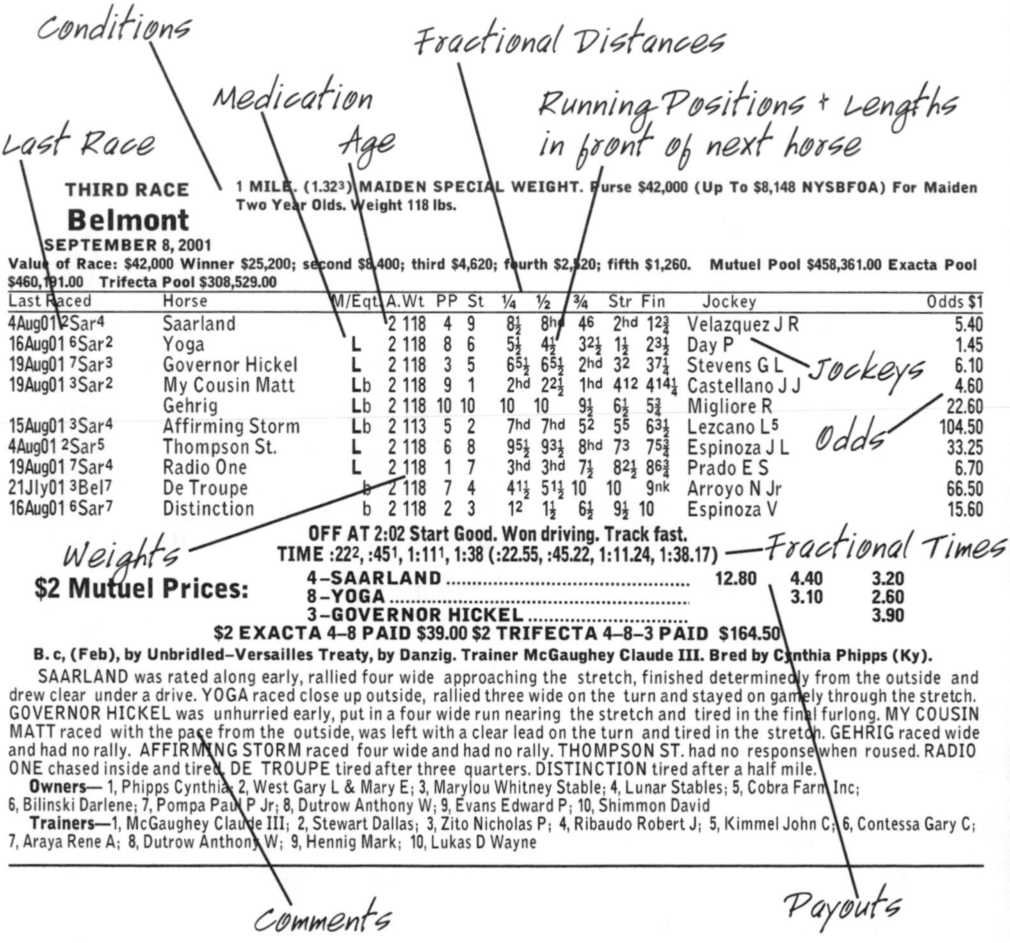
Conditions
Fractional Distances
Medication
Running Positions + Lengths in front of next horse
Last Race
Age
Jockeys
Odds
Weights
Fractional Times
Comments
Payouts

THIRD RACE **1 MILE. (1.32³) MAIDEN SPECIAL WEIGHT. Purse $42,000 (Up To $8,148 NYSBFOA) For Maiden Two Year Olds. Weight 118 lbs.**

Belmont

SEPTEMBER 8, 2001

Value of Race: $42,000 Winner $25,200; second $8,400; third $4,620; fourth $2,520; fifth $1,260. Mutuel Pool $458,361.00 Exacta Pool $460,191.00 Trifecta Pool $308,529.00

Last Raced	Horse	M/Eqt.	A. Wt	PP	St	¼	½	¾	Str	Fin	Jockey	Odds $1
4Aug01 2Sar4	Saarland		2 118	4	9	8½	8hd	46	2hd	12¾	Velazquez J R	5.40
16Aug01 6Sar2	Yoga	L	2 118	8	6	5½	4½	32½	1½	23½	Day P	1.45
19Aug01 7Sar3	Governor Hickel	L	2 118	3	5	65½	65½	2hd	32	37¼	Stevens G L	6.10
19Aug01 3Sar2	My Cousin Matt	Lb	2 118	9	1	2hd	22½	1hd	412	414¼	Castellano J J	4.60
	Gehrig	Lb	2 118	10	10	10	10	9½	6½	5¾	Migliore R	22.60
15Aug01 3Sar4	Affirming Storm	Lb	2 113	5	2	7hd	7hd	52	55	63½	Lezcano L5	104.50
4Aug01 2Sar5	Thompson St.	L	2 118	6	8	95½	93½	8hd	73	75¾	Espinoza J L	33.25
19Aug01 7Sar4	Radio One	L	2 118	1	7	3hd	3hd	7½	82½	86¾	Prado E S	6.70
21Jly01 3Bel7	De Troupe	b	2 118	7	4	41½	51½	10	10	9nk	Arroyo N Jr	66.50
16Aug01 6Sar7	Distinction	b	2 118	2	3	12	1½	6½	9½	10	Espinoza V	15.60

OFF AT 2:02 Start Good. Won driving. Track fast.
TIME :22², :45¹, 1:11¹, 1:38 (:22.55, :45.22, 1:11.24, 1:38.17)

$2 Mutuel Prices:

4–SAARLAND	12.80	4.40	3.20
8–YOGA		3.10	2.60
3–GOVERNOR HICKEL			3.90

$2 EXACTA 4–8 PAID $39.00 $2 TRIFECTA 4–8–3 PAID $164.50

B. c, (Feb), by Unbridled–Versailles Treaty, by Danzig. Trainer McGaughey Claude III. Bred by Cynthia Phipps (Ky).

SAARLAND was rated along early, rallied four wide approaching the stretch, finished determinedly from the outside and drew clear under a drive. YOGA raced close up outside, rallied three wide on the turn and stayed on gamely through the stretch. GOVERNOR HICKEL was unhurried early, put in a four wide run nearing the stretch and tired in the final furlong. MY COUSIN MATT raced with the pace from the outside, was left with a clear lead on the turn and tired in the stretch. GEHRIG raced wide and had no rally. AFFIRMING STORM raced four wide and had no rally. THOMPSON ST. had no response when roused. RADIO ONE chased inside and tired. DE TROUPE tired after three quarters. DISTINCTION tired after a half mile.

Owners— 1, Phipps Cynthia; 2, West Gary L & Mary E; 3, Marylou Whitney Stable; 4, Lunar Stables; 5, Cobra Farm Inc; 6, Bilinski Darlene; 7, Pompa Paul P Jr; 8, Dutrow Anthony W; 9, Evans Edward P; 10, Shimmon David

Trainers— 1, McGaughey Claude III; 2, Stewart Dallas; 3, Zito Nicholas P; 4, Ribaudo Robert J; 5, Kimmel John C; 6, Contessa Gary C; 7, Araya Rene A; 8, Dutrow Anthony W; 9, Hennig Mark; 10, Lukas D Wayne

As you can see, there is a great deal of relevant information making up a race chart, and, as always, information is only as good as the way it is used. So a good understanding of exactly what is being offered is essential if we are to proceed in dissecting this information and turning it into profitable theories, angles, and edges.

There are great differences between a race-result chart and a horse's past-performance lines. Initially, the information in the race-result charts creates the horse's past-performance lines. However, every feature in the chart is not to be comprehended and considered in the same way when reading the past-performance lines.

For example, in a race chart, the lengths reported with each horse's running position at each point of call reflect only the distance between that horse and the horse directly behind him. On the other hand, the lengths reported in a horse's past-performance lines reflect the total distance behind the leader at that particular point of call.

When this race chart is merged into the DRF database, the information from the chart creates the horse's past-performance line for that race, and the number of lengths off the leader at each point of call are accurately totaled and calculated. Here is an example:

Lengths in front of horse in 9th position

Lengths in front of horse in 5th position

THIRD RACE
Belmont
1 MILE. (1.32³) MAIDEN SPECIAL WEIGHT. Purse $42,000 (Up To $8,148 NYSBFOA) For Maiden Two Year Olds. Weight 118 lbs.

SEPTEMBER 8, 2001

Value of Race: $42,000 Winner $25,200; second $8,400; third $4,620; fourth $2,520; fifth $1,260. Mutuel Pool $458,361.00 Exacta Pool $460,191.00 Trifecta Pool $308,529.00

Last Raced	Horse	M/Eqt.	A.Wt	PP	St	¼	½	¾	Str	Fin	Jockey	Odds $1
4Aug01 2Sar⁴	Saarland		2 118	4	9	8½	8hd	4⁶	2hd	12¾	Velazquez J R	5.40
16Aug01 6Sar²	Yoga	L	2 118	8	6	5½	4½	32½	1½	23½	Day P	1.45
19Aug01 7Sar³	Governor Hickel	L	2 118	3	5	65½	65½	2hd	3²	37¼	Stevens G L	6.10
19Aug01 3Sar²	My Cousin Matt	Lb	2 118	9	1	2hd	22½	1hd	412	414¼	Castellano J J	4.60
	Gehrig	Lb	2 118	10	10	10	10	9½	6½	5¾	Migliore R	22.60
15Aug01 3Sar⁴	Affirming Storm	Lb	2 113	5	2	7hd	7hd	5²	5⁵	63½	Lezcano L⁵	104.50
4Aug01 2Sar⁵	Thompson St.	L	2 118	6	8	95½	93½	8hd	7³	75¾	Espinoza J L	33.25
19Aug01 7Sar⁴	Radio One	L	2 118	1	7	3hd	3hd	7½	82½	86¾	Prado E S	6.70
21Jly01 3Bel⁷	De Troupe	b	2 118	7	4	41½	51½	10	10	9nk	Arroyo N Jr	66.50
16Aug01 6Sar⁷	Distinction	b	2 118	2	3	1²	1½	6½	9½	10	Espinoza V	15.60

OFF AT 2:02 Start Good. Won driving. Track fast.
TIME :22², :45¹, 1:11¹, 1:38 (:22.55, :45.22, 1:11.24, 1:38.17)

$2 Mutuel Prices:
4–SAARLAND 12.80 4.40 3.20
8–YOGA 3.10 2.60
3–GOVERNOR HICKEL 3.90
$2 EXACTA 4–8 PAID $39.00 $2 TRIFECTA 4–8–3 PAID $164.50

B. c, (Feb), by Unbridled–Versailles Treaty, by Danzig. Trainer McGaughey Claude III. Bred by Cynthia Phipps (Ky).

SAARLAND was rated along early, rallied four wide approaching the stretch, finished determinedly from the outside and drew clear under a drive. YOGA raced close up outside, rallied three wide on the turn and stayed on gamely through the stretch. GOVERNOR HICKEL was unhurried early, put in a four wide run nearing the stretch and tired in the final furlong. MY COUSIN MATT raced with the pace from the outside, was left with a clear lead on the turn and tired in the stretch. GEHRIG raced wide and had no rally. AFFIRMING STORM raced four wide and had no rally. THOMPSON ST. had no response when roused. RADIO ONE chased inside and tired. DE TROUPE tired after three quarters. DISTINCTION tired after a half mile.

Owners— 1, Phipps Cynthia; 2, West Gary L & Mary E; 3, Marylou Whitney Stable; 4, Lunar Stables; 5, Cobra Farm Inc; 6, Bilinski Darlene; 7, Pompa Paul P Jr; 8, Dutrow Anthony W; 9, Evans Edward P; 10, Shimmon David

Trainers— 1, McGaughey Claude III; 2, Stewart Dallas; 3, Zito Nicholas P; 4, Ribaudo Robert J; 5, Kimmel John C; 6, Contessa Gary C; 7, Araya Rene A; 8, Dutrow Anthony W; 9, Hennig Mark; 10, Lukas D Wayne

Note that according to the race chart, Saarland was in 8th position after a quarter of a mile had been run, a half-length in front of the horse in 9th place. The past-performance line also reflects that Saarland was in 8th position at that same point of call, but reports that he was 9¾ total lengths off the lead.

This is an important fact to consider while trying to calculate how fast a horse was running at different points of call during a race. Before we can accurately determine just how quickly a horse was traveling, we need to establish the correct number of lengths off the leader at each particular point of call.

Once this information is verified, we can then calculate how fast a horse was running at each point of the race.

Running Positions

Total lengths off leader at each point

1 Saarland

B. c. 2 (Feb)
Sire: **Unbridled** (Fappiano)
Dam: **Versailles Treaty** (Danzig)
Br: **Cynthia Phipps (Ky)**
Tr: **McGaughey Claude III** (13 5 1 3 .38) 2001:(179 38 .21)

Own: **Phipps Cynthia**
Gold, Purple Sleeves And Cap

VELAZQUEZ J R (69 12 10 14 .17) 2001:(1127 235 .21)

122

	Life	2	1	0	0	$27,660	74		D.Fst	1	1	0	0	$25,200	74
	2001	2	1	0	0	$27,660	74		Wet(385)	1	0	0	0	$2,460	58
	2000	0	M	0	0	$0	–		Turf(300)	0	0	0	0	$0	–
	Bel	1	1	0	0	$25,200	74		Dist	0	0	0	0	$0	–

8Sep01-3Bel fst 1 :22² :45¹ 1:11¹ 1:38   Md Sp Wt 42k   74 4 8⁹⅜ 8¹⁰ 4²⅜ 2½ 12¾ Velazquez J R   118   5.40 77-14 Saarland118²¾ Yoga118³¾ Governor Hickel1187¼   4 wide move, driving 10
4Aug01-2Sar my 7f :23 :46³ 1:11⁴ 1:24⁴   Md Sp Wt 41k   58 6 3 7⁴¾ 7⁷¾ 4⁸¼ 4⁷¾ Day P   118   *2.15 73-17 LighteningDehere118¹¼PowrConnction1185¼ Fin/Tb/181   Going well late 9

WORKS: Oct2 Bel 4f fst :47³ B 2/20 Sep19 Bel 4f fst :48¹ B 10/33 Sep2 Sar tr.t 4f fst :48⁴ B 2/15 Aug27 Sar tr.t 4f fst :50¹ B 8/17 Jly29 Sar tr.t 4f fst :50 B 6/16

TRAINER: 2YO(57 .19 $1.72) Dirt(346 .25 $1.62) GrdStk(93 .13 $1.22) Sep27 Bel 5f fst 1:03³ B 26/32 Routes(258 .22 $1.81)

2

GRASS AND DIRT

*T*HERE ARE VAST differences between grass racing and dirt racing, and understanding the nature of each surface is essential in order to successfully interpret exactly what transpired during a race.

Each surface has its own science, logic, and distinctions, which greatly differ from the other's. Because of this, the results of turf races and dirt races have to be interpreted differently and read in a different way, which will essentially either add to or subtract from a horse's state of conditioning.

Due to the contrasts between the two surfaces, jockeys will use different riding styles, and trainers will use different conditioning maneuvers. Basically, both are trying to adapt their skills and methods to the running style that best suits each particular horse as it performs on each racing surface.

For example, grass simply is not a surface conducive to early speed. It is much harder to keep speed going on grass than it is on dirt. Therefore, most jockeys will take back early in grass races, trying to reserve their horses' energy for the stretch run. The majority of top grass riders will tell you that, given the opportunity, they try to tuck in as close as possible to the inner rail in the early stages of a turf race, and they try to keep their horses relaxed. Both of these tactics enable their horses to having something left for the stretch run. Of course if a horse has natural speed, riders say that they will not try and choke a horse back, trying to get him to do something he doesn't want to do.

Another major difference between dirt and turf is that in a turf race, the fastest quarter is usually the last quarter, while the fastest quarter of a dirt race is usually the first quarter. This is due not only to the natural characteristics of each surface, but also to the corresponding differences in riding styles on dirt versus turf.

Dirt racing is a more honest form of racing when talking about speed. Early positioning and tactical speed are far more important and advantageous on dirt. For the most part, a dirt surface will not hinder an early-speed horse as compared to a turf surface. Therefore, early speed and tactical speed play more of a major role in the outcome of dirt races than they do in turf races.

Wet weather affects these surfaces differently as well. When a dirt track gets wet, it tends to favor speed even more. On the other hand, a soggy turf course makes it even tougher for an early-speed type to hold for a win. When grass gets wet, it gets softer and then heavier, causing a horse's foot to sink in deeper.

Wet turf makes it even more difficult than it already is for a horse with natural speed to keep going.

The following illustration shows the body of two race charts. Both races were run at the same distance, but one was run on a dirt surface and the other over the grass. Note that I have added the breakdown of fractions by quarter to the right of the actual race time.

SECOND RACE

Belmont

SEPTEMBER 29, 2001

1 MILE. (1.32³) MAIDEN SPECIAL WEIGHT. Purse $42,000 (Up To $8,148 NYSBFOA) For Maiden Two Year Olds. Weight 118 lbs.

Value of Race: $42,000 Winner $25,200; second $8,400; third $4,620; fourth $2,520; fifth $1,260. Mutuel Pool $384,658.00 Exacta Pool $380,178.00 Quinella Pool $46,676.00 Trifecta Pool $258,621.00

Last Raced	Horse	M/Eqt. A.Wt	PP	St	1/4	1/2	3/4	Str	Fin	Jockey	Odds $1
8Sep01 3Bel2	Yoga	L 2 118	1	6	1¹	1½	2hd	1hd	1¹	Day P	1.80
3Sep01 4Sar5	Stroud	L 2 118	4	5	2hd	2½	1hd	22½	2³¾	Chavez J F	3.10
27Aug01 3Sar3	Maybry's Boy	2 118	3	4	3hd	5¹	5½	3½	3no	Velazquez J R	2.70
27Aug01 3Sar6	Silent Fred	L 2 118	6	3	4½	3hd	4hd	4½	4¹	Nakatani C S	19.10
13Aug01 4Sar5	Justin's Thunder	2 118	8	2	6hd	6hd	65½	5¹½	5³¾	Bridgmohan S X	26.75
23Aug01 2Sar2	Survivor Kippy	Lb 2 118	7	1	5hd	4½	3¹	6¹5	622½	Prado E S	4.70
	Regal Beginning	b 2 118	2	8	76	7¹²	76	78	79½	Migliore R	43.75
8Sep01 5Med4	Head Of State	L 2 118	5	7	8	8	8	8	8	Castellano J J	47.75

OFF AT 1:31 Start Good. Won driving. Track fast.

TIME :234, :474, 1:123, 1:384 (:23.92, :47.82, 1:12.68, 1:38.93) *23⁴ 24 24⁴ 26¹*

$2 Mutuel Prices:

1–YOGA	5.60	3.00	2.30
4–STROUD		4.00	2.80
3–MAYBRY'S BOY			2.60

$2 EXACTA 1–4 PAID $19.20 $2 QUINELLA 1–4 PAID $10.20 $2 TRIFECTA 1 4 3 PAID $45.40

Ch. c, (Mar), by Mt. Livermore–Haven, by Forty Niner. Trainer Stewart Dallas. Bred by Hermitage Farm LLC (Ky).

YOGA argued the pace along the inside, dug in gamely on the rail and was driving under the wire. STROUD argued the pace while between rivals and finished gamely outside. MAYBRY'S BOY raced close up on the rail, was steadied along the inside on the turn and lacked a rally. SILENT FRED contested the pace while between rivals three wide and weakened in the final furlong. JUSTIN'S THUNDER raced close up outside and lacked a rally. SURVIVOR KIPPY argued the pace while four wide and tired in the stretch. REGAL BEGINNING tired after three quarters. HEAD OF STATE had no response when roused and tired.

Owners— 1, West Gary L & Mary E; 2, Pokoik Lee; 3, R C Hill Stable; 4, Conway Dee; 5, Cohen Robert B; 6, Johnson Ted J & Johnson Kim; 7, Lee Lewis & Alan Brodsky; 8, New Walter L

Trainers— 1, Stewart Dallas; 2, Sciacca Gary; 3, McGaughey Claude III; 4, Zito Nicholas P; 5, Johnson Philip G; 6, Bond Harold James; 7, Hennig Mark; 8, Fawkes David

$2 Daily Double (4–1) Paid $57.50; Daily Double Pool $371,378.

SEVENTH RACE

Saratoga

SEPTEMBER 3, 2001

1 MILE (Inner Turf) (1:33³) ALLOWANCE. Purse $46,000 INNER TURF. (Up to $8,924 NYSBFOA) For Three Year Olds And Upward Which Have Never Won Three Races. Three Year Olds 118 lbs.; Older 122 lbs. Non–winners of $26,000 at a mile or over on the turf since June 30 allowed, 2 lbs. (Races where entered for $60,000 or less not considered in allowances). (Preference by condition eligibility).

Value of Race: $46,000 Winner $27,600; second $9,200; third $5,060; fourth $2,760; fifth $1,380. Mutuel Pool $787,651.00 Exacta Pool $741,989.00 Trifecta Pool $518,659.00

Last Raced	Horse	M/Eqt.	A.Wt	PP	St	¼	½	¾	Str	Fin	Jockey	Odds $1
3Aug01 7Sar¹	Krieger	Lb	3 118	2	1	1¹¹⁄₂	1¹⁄₂	1¹⁄₂	1¹¹⁄₂	1²¹⁄₂	Chavez J F	2.20
25Jly01 5Sar¹	Aslaaf	Lb	3 118	8	7	4²¹⁄₂	3hd	2¹⁄₂	2³¹⁄₂	2²²⁄₃	Velazquez J R	3.15
28Jly01 5Sar³	French Envoy	L	5 120	1	2	3hd	4²¹⁄₂	4hd	3hd	3hd	Prado E S	3.40
5Aug01 10Sar¹	Broadway Snowman	L	4 122	9	9	5hd	5¹⁄₂	5hd	5¹⁄₂	4³⁄₄	Migliore R	8.40
9Jun01 9CD⁹	Tarzan Cry-IR		3 116	4	8	8²	7¹⁄₂	7⁴¹⁄₂	7⁴¹⁄₂	5¹⁄₂	Day P	8.90
25Aug01 6Sar⁹	Treasured Gift	L	4 120	5	5	7¹⁄₂	6²¹⁄₂	6²¹⁄₂	6¹⁄₂	6nk	Gryder A T	37.50
23Jun01 7Bel³	Quiet Quest	L	4 120	6	4	2¹⁄₂	2¹	3²	4hd	7²¹⁄₂	Samyn J L	7.00
27Jly01 9AP⁸	Lake Storm	Lf	4 115	3	3	6¹¹⁄₂	8hd	8¹⁄₂	8⁴¹⁄₂	8⁶¹⁄₄	Lezcano L⁵	74.50
10Aug01 9Sar⁷	Flake O	f	3 116	7	6	9	9	9	9	9	Bridgmohan S X	46.00

OFF AT 4:19 Start Good. Won ridden out. Course good.
TIME :24, :47³, 1:11³, 1:34⁴ (:24.10, :47.63, 1:11.68, 1:34.84)   :24 :23³ :24 :23¹

$2 Mutuel Prices:

3–KRIEGER	6.40	3.80	3.00
9–ASLAAF		4.10	3.00
1–FRENCH ENVOY			2.90

$2 EXACTA 3–9 PAID $21.40 $2 TRIFECTA 3–9–1 PAID $58.00

Ch. c, (Feb), by Lord At War*Arg–Abigailthewife, by Affirmed. Trainer Orseno Joseph. Bred by Adena Springs (Ky).

KRIEGER quickly showed in front, set the pace, responded when asked and was ridden out to the wire. ASLAAF raced close up outside, rallied three wide and finished gamely. FRENCH ENVOY was rated along inside and lacked a solid finishing kick. BROADWAY SNOWMAN was rated along outside, raced wide and had no impact on the outcome. TARZAN CRY (IRE) was rated along inside, came wide for the drive and lacked a rally. TREASURED GIFT raced inside and had no rally. QUIET QUEST raced with the pace for three quarters and tired. LAKE STORM was outrun. FLAKE O tired.

Owners— 1, Stronach Stable; 2, al Maktoum Sheikh Maktoum; 3, Cowan Marjorie & Irving M; 4, Appleton Arthur I; 5, Mansell Stables Rio Adventura Stabl; 6, Buckram Oak Farm; 7, Ritzenberg Mrs Grace E; 8, James Lake Lee Lake Gerald Sabies &; 9, Brida Dennis J & Stevens Win

Trainers—1, Orseno Joseph; 2, McLaughlin Kiaran P; 3, Tesher Howard M; 4, Clement Christophe; 5, Walden W Elliott; 6, Moubarak Mohammed; 7, Turner William H Jr; 8, Lake James; 9, Brida Dennis J

Scratched— Conormara (1Jly01 CUR¹⁷)

$2 Pick Three (1–4–3) Paid $291.00; Pick Three Pool $133,114.

The first quarter of the dirt race was the fastest quarter recorded, while the last quarter of the grass race was the quickest. This takes on great significance while keeping charts, because you want to make accurate assessments of individual efforts as judged through the quality of the fractional calls of time.

Trying to decipher whether a race or individual effort was better or worse than the norm will be of tremendous importance. This will aid in detecting good efforts as well as poor efforts in addition to tipping us off to potential key races.

3

UNDERSTANDING PACE

FOR THE PURPOSES of keeping race charts, one doesn't need any prior knowledge of a pace formula, a pace program, pace angles, or any other type of pace-related numerology. All that is required is a basic understanding of what pace actually is and how it develops within the body of a race.

Once understood, this concept will provide you with a deeper insight into horses' running lines and the fractional calls of time within these running lines. This insight will then aid in recognizing a high-quality effort and, just as importantly, a poor-quality one. This knowledge will also enable you to judge performances and abilities much more easily and accurately.

A definition of pace could be explained as a rate or measurement of movement. That's simple enough to understand, but trying to judge pace can be very tricky.

Let's begin with a distance of two furlongs. In general, a horse deemed to have a very good turn of early speed would be able to run two furlongs in 22 seconds, an average of 11 seconds per furlong. If the horse continued on this same pace he would run three furlongs in 33 seconds and four furlongs in 44 seconds—a pace that would be considered lightning fast, but still quite possible for a Thoroughbred to sustain up to this distance.

If he continued running at this same pace, he would record five furlongs in 55 seconds, which is almost impossible. I say "almost" because if a surface is yielding lightning-fast times, it could be done, though most likely with a ton of help from the surface and/or track condition, such as a frozen track or a baked, rock-hard turf course.

For distances over four furlongs and up to $6\frac{1}{2}$ furlongs, it is more reasonable to calculate that a horse can maintain a pace of 12 seconds per furlong. This is not to say that a horse can't run the last furlong of a route race in 11 seconds, but in order to do so, he would have had to run at a slower pace earlier, expending less energy.

Sprint races are less complex than routes. The pace of a sprint race is usually faster than that of a route race simply because of the difference in distances. Pace puzzles begin when the basic sprinter or speed type is asked to stretch out.

When an early-speed type breaks from the gate while being asked to go farther than his normal distance, the rider most likely will not gun the horse as hard as he usually would to establish early tactical position. Instead of getting a first quarter in 22 seconds and a half-mile in somewhere around 45 seconds, the horse will most likely be rated a little more in the hope that he will last longer on the lead.

Suppose this same horse goes out in fractions of 23 and 47 seconds. The question now is how much farther he can last at today's slower pace. Since he is going slower, he should be able to go longer. We know he is capable of producing quicker early fractions, but how much more energy he will have stored by going slower early on?

The answer lies in each horse's own abilities, and it is our job as handicappers to know just what he has in the tank before we wager on this race. Furthermore, we must reason how quick today's pace scenario figures to be, and whether the early-speed types in this field will still be around at the finish.

Studying a horse's history and interpreting each race can help us try to assess just how good he is and how much ability he brings with him. By doing this, one will get a feeling of strength stemming from the quality of fractions and final time each horse has created.

Clearly it is a sign of strength when a horse can maintain a fast pace over a distance of ground. The faster the pace and the longer the distance, the greater the quality of this particular horse's ability. In fact, ultimately, a horse's true class can be measured in time over a distance.

To fully understand the values of pace, one must get a feeling of strength from reading a horse's running lines. Careful analysis of these should help us weigh how fast a horse actually is. Perhaps the simplest way to read a horse's running line is to look at it as a graph. Let's use the following running line as an example of looking at a horse's running line like a graph as we highlight it on my pace chart.

1⅛ miles		:23	:46	1:10	1:35	1:47
Fractional Breakdown	:23	:23	:24	:25	:12	= 1:47

2	3	4	4.5	5	5.5	6	6.5	7	7.5	mile	1m 40/yd	1m 70/yd	1 1/16	1 1/8	1 3/16	1 1/4	1 3/8	1 1/2
:20																		
1																		
2																		
3																		
4																		
:21	:31	:42	:48	:54	1:00	1:06	1:12	1:19	1:25	1:32	1:35	1:37	1:39	1:45	1:52	1:58	2:11	2:24
1	1	1	1	1	1	1	1	1	1	1								
2	2	2	2	2	2	2	2	2	2	2								
3	3	3	3	3	3	3	3	3	3	3								
4	4	4	4	4	4	4	4	4	4	4								
	:32	:43	:49	:55	1:01	1:07	1:13	1:20	1:26	1:33	1:36	1:38	1:40	1:46	1:53	1:59	2:12	2:25
	1	1	1	1	1	1	1	1	1	1								
	2	2	2	2	2	2	2	2	2	2								
	3	3	3	3	3	3	3	3	3	3								
	4	4	4	4	4	4	4	4	4	4								
:22	:33	:44	:50	:56	1:02	1:08	1:14	1:21	1:27	1:34	1:37	1:39	1:41	1:47	1:54	2:00	2:13	2:26
1	1	1	1	1	1	1	1	1	1	1								
2	2	2	2	2	2	2	2	2	2	2								
3	3	3	3	3	3	3	3	3	3	3								
4	4	4	4	4	4	4	4	4	4	4								
	:34	:45	:51	:57	1:03	1:09	1:15	1:22	1:28	1:35	1:38	1:40	1:42	1:48	1:55	2:01	2:14	2:27
	1	1	1	1	1	1	1	1	1	1								
	2	2	2	2	2	2	2	2	2	2								
	3	3	3	3	3	3	3	3	3	3								
	4	4	4	4	4	4	4	4	4	4								
:23	:35	:46	:52	:58	1:04	1:10	1:16	1:23	1:29	1:36	1:39	1:41	1:43	1:49	1:56	2:02	2:15	2:28
1	1	1	1	1	1	1	1	1	1	1								
2	2	2	2	2	2	2	2	2	2	2								
3	3	3	3	3	3	3	3	3	3	3								
4	4	4	4	4	4	4	4	4	4	4								
	:36	:47	:53	:59	1:05	1:11	1:17	1:24	1:30	1:37	1:40	1:42	1:44	1:50	1:57	2:03	2:16	2:29
	1	1	1	1	1	1	1	1	1	1								
	2	2	2	2	2	2	2	2	2	2								
	3	3	3	3	3	3	3	3	3	3								
	4	4	4	4	4	4	4	4	4	4								
:24	:37	:48	:54	1:00	1:06	1:12	1:18	1:25	1:31	1:38	1:41	1:43	1:45	1:51	1:58	2:04	2:17	2:30
1	1	1	1	1	1	1	1	1	1	1								
2	2	2	2	2	2	2	2	2	2	2								
3	3	3	3	3	3	3	3	3	3	3								
4	4	4	4	4	4	4	4	4	4	4								
	:38	:49	:55	1:01	1:07	1:13	1:19	1:26	1:32	1:39	1:42	1:44	1:46	1:52	1:59	2:05	2:18	2:31
	1	1	1	1	1	1	1	1	1	1								
	2	2	2	2	2	2	2	2	2	2								
	3	3	3	3	3	3	3	3	3	3								
	4	4	4	4	4	4	4	4	4	4								
:25	:39	:50	:56	1:02	1:08	1:14	1:20	1:27	1:33	1:40	1:43	1:45	1:47	1:53	2:00	2:06	2:19	2:32

Using this par/pace chart like a graph, I mapped out the sample running line and illustrated it on the chart. Note that the pace of the race actually increases as the distance gets longer. Even though the number of seconds between each furlong got slower, the pace values still increased to a higher degree.

This is an example of one of the basic principles of pace in Thoroughbred racing. Since we realized earlier that a horse usually can't maintain a pace of 11 seconds per furlong for five furlongs, it's a given that as the distance increases, the time it takes for an individual horse to get through each furlong usually gets slower.

We had already established this fact while creating the guidelines of how fast a horse should be able to run each furlong in relation to the distance that he had already run. These guidelines were created after studying the past performances of some of the greatest Thoroughbreds that ever ran. The track records of most major racecourses were also studied in creating these guidelines.

I included my pace chart at this time only to illustrate, and hopefully help you understand a little more easily, how pace should be understood. As time goes by and you work with horses' running lines along with the par/pace chart, you will notice that the better horses usually make the graph go upward, especially on final time.

This is about as deep as you need to go concerning pace to fully understand the concept in relation to keeping charts.

While keeping charts with regard to pace, it is advisable first to break all fractional calls of time down to quarters (two furlongs).

Of course, if there are fractions of time that can't be broken down into quarters, then an eighth (one furlong) or a sixteenth (half a furlong) will do the trick.

To establish the quality of the fractional times within a route race, use the guideline that the first quarter should be run in 23 $\frac{2}{5}$ seconds or less. Anything slower would be ordinary.

For the remaining parts of route races, the guideline will be to highlight any quarter fraction that was run in 24 seconds or less. We should also highlight any eighth that was run in 12 seconds or less and any sixteenth that was run in six seconds or less. The breakdown for routes after the first quarter should be 12 seconds per furlong and six seconds for a half-furlong (a sixteenth).

While trying to determine the quality of a sprint race, the guideline for the first quarter requires that it should be run in 22 $\frac{3}{5}$ seconds or less. For the remaining portion of this sprint race, we should highlight any other remaining quarter fraction run in 23 seconds or less and, here again, any eighth of a mile done in 12 seconds or less.

These fractional-breakdown rules and guidelines should be used for both turf and dirt races. Even though racing on each surface differs strategically, the fractional and final-time break-downs should still be regarded in the same ways for record keeping and for deciphering quality efforts.

For the purpose of charting races, after breaking down the fractional calls of time, we then proceed by highlighting each fraction that was within the guidelines we just discussed. The next step would be to highlight the horses that were in contention at each of these highlighted fractional calls of time. By *contention,* we mean that we highlight horses that were close to the lead at each call.

The goal now is to discover a horse that has given a better than ordinary effort for a major part of the race. This is easily accomplished due to the breakdown of fractional times and the segmented recording of each horse's performance on the race-result charts.

By going through these steps, you might uncover a horse that will have an edge over the field he is to face next time out. On the other hand, even if such a horse is not present, we still might uncover some other valuable racing information.

Perhaps we might have discovered that a horse made a seemingly average middle move where he gained four lengths from the start to the three-quarter mark. After analyzing the fractional-time breakdowns, we realize that this middle move was made into the teeth of a quarter-mile fraction in 23 seconds. This seemingly ordinary middle move is now far better than first thought, and might tip us off to a horse that is about to run a huge race.

This is why the fractional breakdowns of each race and the fractional guidelines for a running line have great importance. They emphasize how to judge quality with regard to pace.

The following illustration is an example of a highlighted chart denoting pace analysis and performance at each point of call:

SEVENTH RACE
Belmont
OCTOBER 14, 2001

1⅛ MILES. (Inner Turf)(1.45^{3}) 9th Running of THE PEBBLES HANDICAP. Grade III. FIRST DIVISION. Purse $100,000. (Up to $19,400 NYSBFOA). A HANDICAP FOR FILLIES, THREE YEARS OLD. By subscription of $100 each, which should accompany the nomination; $500 to pass the entry box; $500 to start, with $100,000 added. The added money and all fees to be divided 60% to the winner, 20% to second, 11% to third, 6% to fourth and 3% to fifth. Trophies will be presented to the winning owner, trainer and jockey. The New York Racing Association reserves the right to transfer this race to the Main Track. In the event that this race is taken off the turf, it may be subject to downgrading upon review by the Graded Stakes Committee. Closed Saturday, September 29, 2001 with 42 Nominations .

Value of Race: $110,100 Winner $66,060; second $22,020; third $12,111; fourth $6,606; fifth $3,303. Mutuel Pool $387,067.00 Exacta Pool $316,772.00 Trifecta Pool $238,173.00

Last Raced	Horse	M/Eqt.	A.Wt	PP	St	¼	½	¾	Str	Fin	Jockey	Odds $1
12May01 ^{9}CD^{3}	Heads Will Roll-GB	L	3 115	6	7	$5^{\frac{1}{2}}$	$5^{2\frac{1}{2}}$	5^{2}	$1^{1\frac{1}{2}}$	1^{1}	Prado E S	2.15
23Sep01 ^{7}Del^{2}	New Economy	L	3 114	7	5	8	8	8	3^{hd}	$2^{\frac{1}{2}}$	Dominguez R A	16.00
23Sep01 ^{7}Del^{1}	Salty You	L	3 115	1	2	$2^{1\frac{1}{2}}$	$3^{2\frac{1}{2}}$	3^{hd}	$4^{\frac{1}{2}}$	$3^{\frac{3}{4}}$	Velazquez J R	5.40
22Sep01 ^{10}Med^{1}	[D]Stylish	b	3 116	5	3	$4^{2\frac{1}{2}}$	$4^{1\frac{1}{2}}$	$4^{2\frac{1}{2}}$	$2^{\frac{1}{2}}$	$4^{3\frac{1}{4}}$	Stevens G L	4.80
26Sep01 ^{8}Bel^{3}	Fiddle		3 115	4	4	$6^{2\frac{1}{2}}$	$6^{\frac{1}{2}}$	7^{2}	$6^{1\frac{1}{2}}$	$5^{2\frac{3}{4}}$	Arroyo N Jr	7.90
9Aug01 ^{8}Sar^{5}	Zahwah	Lb	3 113	8	6	$7^{1\frac{1}{2}}$	7^{5}	6^{hd}	7^{6}	$6^{10\frac{1}{4}}$	Castellano J J	22.60
9Sep01 ^{9}Bel^{3}	Wander Mom	Lb	3 116	3	8	$3^{2\frac{1}{2}}$	2^{3}	1^{hd}	$5^{\frac{1}{2}}$	$7^{\frac{1}{2}}$	Gryder A T	2.45
30Sep01 ^{7}Bel^{6}	Takeiteasyedye	Lb	3 114	2	1	$1^{\frac{1}{2}}$	1^{hd}	2^{2}	8	8	Castillo H Jr	54.50

[D]–Stylish disqualified and placed 5th.

OFF AT 4:08 Start Good. Won driving. Course firm.

TIME :24^{2}, :47^{1}, 1:10^{2}, 1:35^{1}, 1:47^{3} (:24.42, :47.39, 1:10.57, 1:35.31, 1:47.75)

242 224 231 244 122

$2 Mutuel Prices:

6–HEADS WILL ROLL–GB	6.30	4.20	3.40
7–NEW ECONOMY		13.20	8.40
1–SALTY YOU			5.60

$2 EXACTA 6–7 PAID $78.50 $2 TRIFECTA 6–7–1 PAID $375.00

Dk. b. or br. f, (Mar), by Efisio*GB–Crazy For You*GB, by Blakeney*GB. Trainer Frankel Robert. Bred by Kingwood Stud Ltd (GB).

HEADS WILL ROLL (GB) was rated along early, rallied four wide approaching the stretch, drew clear when roused and was driving under the wire. NEW ECONOMY was outrun early, came wide into the stretch and finished gamely outside to earn the place award. SALTY YOU raced close up inside, angled out into the stretch and finished gamely while between rivals. STYLISH was steadied along the inside on the first turn, rallied three wide on the second turn and finished well. FIDDLE was taken up along the inside on the first turn and was steadied along the inside in upper stretch. ZAHWAH was outrun early, rallied three wide on the second turn and lacked a solid finishing kick. WANDER MOM showed speed while in hand, came in after her saddle slipped on the first turn, argued the pace and tired in the stretch. TAKEITEASYEDYE argued the pace for three quarters and tired. Following a stewards' inquiry into the run around the first turn, STYLISH was disqualified from fourth position and placed fifth.

Owners— 1, Amerman John W & Amerman Jerome; 2, Evans Robert S; 3, Lael Stables; 4, The Thoroughbred Corporation; 5, Shields Joseph V Jr; 6, Godolphin Inc; 7, Carrion Jaime S; 8, Beecher Aaron

Trainers—1, Frankel Robert; 2, Motion H Graham; 3, Matz Michael R; 4, Mott William I; 5, Jerkens H Allen; 6, Suroor Saeed bin; 7, Plesa Edward Jr; 8, Gullo Gary P

Scratched— Summer Colony (23Sep01 ^{6}BEL^{1})

$2 Pick Three (4–3–6) Paid $117.50: Pick Three Pool $75.008.

After establishing the fractional breakdown of the race by quarters, note that the quickest quarter run was the second quarter in 22⅘ seconds. The horses in contention at that point were Takiteasyedye, who was dueling for the early lead; Wander Mom, who was in second position, a head off the lead; Salty You, who was three lengths behind in third, and Stylish, who was another 2½ lengths back in fourth position.

The rest of the fractions were nothing special, but it is pretty evident who might have run the best race pace-wise. Of the four horses that were in contention during the quickest part of the race, Salty You was able to sustain a bigger effort and finish ahead of the other pace rivals in third.

This is not to say that Salty You is our automatic horse for next time out. What this does mean is that Salty You seemingly ran the best race pace-wise in today's field, but of course we will still have to handicap the past performances next time out and see how and if Salty You figures to improve off today's effort.

We must also read how she fits into her next start from a pace, class, and distance perspective. After all, who knows how good that field will be?

We also have three other horses highlighted on this same chart, which could mean that each horse is improving form-wise. Perhaps Stylish had her chances greatly compromised by being steadied early in the race. Perhaps when Wander Mom's saddle slipped she lost her best chance for victory.

At this point we don't want to rule anyone out. Our goal right now is to highlight the best performances from a pace standpoint and make the information given work for us in the best way possible.

In this race it seems that Salty You gave the best overall pace performance while a few others also ran well during the quickest part of the race. Keep it simple when gathering information so that when you go back and look at this chart some weeks later, you understand exactly what you meant when you created these notes.

In the following race chart it becomes pretty obvious that the best part of the race occurred early on. The breakdown is as follows: $22\,^4/_5$; $22\,^2/_5$; $24\,^2/_5$; and $25\,^1/_5$ seconds.

EIGHTH RACE

Aqueduct

NOVEMBER 29, 2001

1 MILE. (1.32²) ALLOWANCE. Purse $56,000 (Up To $10,864 NYSBFOA) For Three Year Olds And Upward Which Have Not Won Either $5,000 Three Times Other Than Maiden, Claiming, Starter, Or Restricted Since April 1 Or Which Have Never Won Four Races Other Than Maiden, Claiming, Starter, Or Restricted. Three Year Olds 121 lbs.; Older 123 lbs. Non-winners of $30,000 since June 1 allowed, 2 lbs. $32,000 in 2000–01, 4 lbs. $28,000 twice in 2000–01, 6 lbs. (Maiden, claiming, or starter races not considered in allowances).

Value of Race: $56,000 Winner $33,600; second $11,200; third $6,160; fourth $3,360; fifth $1,680.   Mutuel Pool $260,729.00 Exacta Pool $239,801.00   Trifecta Pool $164,394.00

Last Raced	Horse	M/Eqt.	A.Wt	PP	St	¼	½	¾	Str	Fin	Jockey	Odds $1
19Jly01 HC¹	Franbulo-CH	Lf	5 117	1	6	8	8	7¹¹⁄₂	2ʰᵈ	1⁴	Toscano P R	5.10
15Jly01 4Bel⁶	Company Approval	L	5 121	8	3	5¹⁄₂	6⁵	5¹⁄₂	4¹⁄₂	2³⁄₄	Castellano J J	9.70
8Oct01 7Del⁴	Durmiente-CH	L	7 116	4	7	7⁶	7⁷	6³¹⁄₂	5ʰᵈ	3¹¹⁄₂	Pimentel J⁵	4.10
31Oct01 8Aqu⁶	Dayton Flyer	Lb	3 115	7	2	2²	3²¹⁄₂	3¹⁄₂	6¹⁄₂	4ʰᵈ	Bridgmohan S X	4.90
19Oct01 8Med⁶	Dash 'n Dance	Lb	3 117	3	8	6⁷	4ʰᵈ	4¹¹⁄₂	3ʰᵈ	5ʰᵈ	Davis R G	3.80
21Oct01 6Del¹	Country Only	Lf	4 121	2	5	4²¹⁄₂	2¹⁄₂	2¹⁄₂	1¹⁄₂	6⁴¹⁄₄	Velazquez J R	3.15
9Nov01 5Aqu⁸	Presente Senor-CHI	Lb	5 118	6	1	1³	1¹	1¹¹⁄₂	7⁸	7⁵	Lezcano L⁵	38.25
12Nov01 8Aqu¹⁰	Fire King	Lf	8 121	5	4	3ʰᵈ	5ʰᵈ	8	8	8	Gryder A T	12.80

OFF AT 3:48 Start Good. Won driving. Track fast.

TIME :22⁴, :45¹, 1:09³, 1:34⁴ (:22.80, :45.21, 1:09.67, 1:34.80)

$2 Mutuel Prices:

1–FRANBULO–CH	12.20	6.40	4.90
8–COMPANY APPROVAL		9.70	5.80
4–DURMIENTE–CH			3.40

$2 EXACTA 1–8 PAID $156.00 $2 TRIFECTA 1–8–4 PAID $610.00

Dk. b. or br. h, by Hussonet–Seminola*Chi, by Mr. Long. Trainer Serey Juan. Bred by Haras Carampangue (Chi).

FRANBULO (CHI) was outrun early, advanced inside on the turn, swung wide into the stretch, finished strongly from the outside and was going away late, driving. COMPANY APPROVAL was hustled outside, rallied four wide and finished gamely despite his rider having lost his whip in upper stretch. DURMIENTE (CHI) was outrun early, rallied inside on the turn, came wide for the drive and was in tight quarters between rivals in the stretch. DAYTON FLYER chased three wide and was in tight quarters between rivals in the stretch. DASH 'N DANCE raced inside and lacked a rally. COUNTRY ONLY raced with the pace along the inside and tired in the final furlong. PRESENTE SENOR (CHI) quickly showed in front, set the pace for three quarters and tired. FIRE KING tired after showing brief speed.

Owners— 1, Viejo Perro Stud; 2, Siegel Samantha Mace & Jan; 3, La Marca Stable; 4, Sabine Stable & Kelly Robert; 5, Schosberg Paul A; 6, Binn Morton & Marisol; 7, Lamarque William G; 8, Englander Richard A

Trainers— 1, Serey Juan; 2, Dutrow Richard E Jr; 3, Klesaris Robert P; 4, Barbara Robert; 5, Schosberg Richard; 6, Morales Carlos J; 7, Dupps Kristina; 8, Lake Scott A

$2 Pick Six (3–8–11–8–3–1) 6
Correct Paid $28,115.00; Pick Six Pool $46,859. $2 Pick Six (3–8–11–8–3–1) 5
Correct Paid $133.50

After highlighting the horses that were in contention throughout the better parts of this race we learn that Presente Senor battled on the lead while Dayton Flyer, Country Only, and Fire King scrambled to chase him through quick opening splits.

In fact, at the three-quarter mark, there were only three horses in contention for the lead—Presente Senor, Country Only, and Dayton Flyer. The rest of the field's performances were not worth noting as far as pace is concerned.

NINTH RACE
Belmont
SEPTEMBER 9, 2001

1⅛ MILES. (Inner Turf)(1.45^3) 23rd Running of THE GARDEN CITY BREEDERS' CUP HANDICAP. Grade I. Purse $250,000. (Includes $100,000 BC – Breeders' Cup).(Plus up to $38,500 NYSBFOA). A HANDICAP FOR THREE YEAR OLD FILLIES. (Includes $100,000 from Breeders' Cup Fund for cup nominees only). By subscription of $150 each, which should accompany the nomination; $750 to pass the entry box; $750 additional to start. The NYRA purse to be divided 60% to the winner, 20% to second, 11% to third, 6% to fourth and 3% to fifth. Breeders' Cup Fund monies also correspondingly divided provided a Breeders' Cup nominee has finished in an awarded position. Any Breeders' Cup Fund monies not awarded will revert back to the Fund. In the event the Garden City Breeders' Cup overfills, preference will be given to Breeders' Cup nominees only of equal racing quality or weight assignment. A trophy to winning owner given by Breeders' Cup Ltd. The New York Racing Association will present trophies to the winning trainer and jockey. The New York Racing Association reserves the right to transfer this race to the Main Track. In the event that this race is taken off the turf, it may be subject to downgrading upon review by the Graded Stakes Committee. Closed Saturday, August 25, 2001 with 43 Nominations.

Value of Race: $244,000 Winner $150,000; second $50,000; third $27,500; fourth $9,000; fifth $7,500. Mutuel Pool $541,440.00 Exacta Pool $444,928.00 Trifecta Pool $393,267.00

Last Raced	Horse	M/Eqt.	A.Wt	PP	St	¼	½	¾	Str	Fin	Jockey	Odds $1
18Aug01 8Dmr4	Voodoo Dancer	L	3 120	3	3	5½	6hd	5½	2½	14¾	Nakatani C S	1.05
20Aug01 7Sar4	Shooting Party	L	3 113	10	6	12	11½	11	1½	2¾	Samyn J L	a-13.10
20Aug01 8Sar2	Wander Mom	Lb	3 116	2	4	2½	3hd	41	35½	31¾	Gryder A T	9.50
2Aug01 Goo2	Sheppard's Watch-GB	L	3 116	9	10	10	10	8hd	4½	41	Migliore R	7.90
30Jly01 8Sar5	Fiddle		3 116	6	2	7hd	8½	7hd	6hd	5hd	Espinoza J L	a-13.10
20Aug01 8Sar8	Owsley		3 115	7	1	6hd	7½	61½	52½	61½	Prado E S	7.70
20Aug01 9Sar1	Ellie's Moment	L	3 115	5	8	4hd	5½	10	9hd	72½	Velazquez J R	5.50
20Aug01 8Sar7	Light Dancer	Lbf	3 117	8	7	8½	4½	3hd	8hd	8nk	Rivera J A II	15.60
24Aug01 Bad2	Mistic Sun-GB	L	3 115	1	9	9½	9hd	91	71½	91¾	Smith M E	40.75
21Jly01 8Del1	Zonk	L	3 114	4	5	31½	2hd	2hd	10	10	Velez J A Jr	18.80

a–Coupled: Shooting Party and Fiddle.

OFF AT 5:40 Start Good. Won driving. Course firm. 24 24^2 23^3 24

TIME :24, :48^2, 1:12, 1:36, 1:47^3 (:24.14, :48.51, 1:12.13, 1:36.17, 1:47.69) 11^3

$2 Mutuel Prices:				
	4–VOODOO DANCER	**4.10**	**3.00**	**2.40**
	1A–SHOOTING PARTY (a–entry)		**8.70**	**4.60**
	3–WANDER MOM			**3.30**

$2 EXACTA 4–1 PAID $33.40 $2 TRIFECTA 4–1–3 PAID $168.00

B. f, (Apr), by Kingmambo–Zuri, by Danzig. Trainer Clement Christophe. Bred by Lazy E Ranch Inc (Ky).

VOODOO DANCER was bumped at the start, was rated along early, advanced inside on the second turn, came wide into the stretch, took off when asked for run and drew away quickly under a hand ride. SHOOTING PARTY quickly showed in front, set the pace along the inside and stayed on gamely to earn the place award. WANDER MOM raced close up inside while in hand, responded when roused and stayed on well to the finish. SHEPPARD'S WATCH (GB) was outrun early, rallied five wide on the second turn and finished well outside. FIDDLE was rated along early, raced wide and had no rally. OWSLEY was rated outside, raced wide on both turns and had no response when roused. ELLIE'S MOMENT raced close up while between rivals and tired. LIGHT DANCER chased the pace while three wide and tired after the opening three quarters. MISTIC SUN (GB) raced inside and lacked a rally. ZONK chased the pace while between rivals and tired.

Owners— 1, Green Hills Farm; 2, Shields Joseph V Jr; 3, Carrion Jaime S; 4, Lael Stables; 5, Shields Joseph V Jr; 6, Hancock III Arthur B; 7, Phillips Joan G & John W; 8, Loewenstein Harvey J Criollo Barbar; 9, Tanaka Gary A; 10, Fox Hill Farms Inc

Trainers—1, Clement Christophe; 2, Jerkens H Allen; 3, Plesa Edward Jr; 4, Clement Christophe; 5, Jerkens H Allen; 6, Schulhofer Flint S; 7, Toner James J; 8, Crillo Manuel; 9, Schutz Andreas; 10, Servis John C.

Acknowledging that the final fraction is the quickest, we also must realize that there are still three quarters of the race that were run in 24 seconds or faster. This being the case, the next step is to go through each fractional call of time and establish which horses were in contention at each stage.

I circled the running positions of the horses that were in contention at each point of the race that was run in 24 seconds or better. Note that the highlighted horses' names earn the most denotations when it comes to pace analysis. Shooting Party and Wander Mom might have run the best races, while Voodoo Dancer took advantage of the quick pace scenario by rating off the early lead and Sheppard's Watch put in a five-wide run on the turn for home.

Breaking down a race this way makes reading a race chart more comprehensive and provides a better understanding of just how the race was run and how it was won or lost. Terms like "coming out of a good race" and "the first part was quick," along with "he finished fast" can easily be comprehended and proved one way or another by breaking down a race fractionally.

4

REDEFINING
A KEY RACE

ONE OF THE biggest misconceptions regarding a key race is the notion that at least two horses have to come out of it to win their next starts. I have always felt that this definition can be very misleading.

For instance, let's say that no horses come back and win in their next starts after exiting from the same race. According to the previous definition, this race could never be considered a key race. But now let's suppose four horses come out of this very same race and in their next starts they all run huge races to lose by either a head or a nose, all finishing second. Wouldn't you have to consider this a key race?

Three years ago I was charting a day's card and I came across a route race I thought might become a key race because it was run about two seconds faster from the start to the three-quarter point than the other races on the same card. The first horse out of this projected key race, one who had dueled for the lead before tiring, ran back and finished second. I began thinking I might be on to something good.

I then waited for the next horse that gave a similar speed type of effort in this potential key race to be entered back. A week later, the second horse exiting this race came back and went off at odds of 22-1. He also finished second. I had invested in the horse to win and place, but I also backed him up in an exacta with the next logical horse, and that exacta returned $140.

What was amazing about this key race was that four horses came out of it and all returned to run second in their next starts. Ever since, my personal definition of a key race has become a race where at least two horses come out and return with measurable big efforts.

A key goal when considering a key race is identifying it as being key before the betting public does, thereby ensuring yourself of a solid price on the horse or horses you are tracking.

Spotting a key race through performance is done by noting today's finish positions for the top four finishers in any given race, then going back to each horse's prior start and marking today's finish position on that previous race chart. By doing this with each race chart, you will know exactly which horses came out of any given race and performed well in their next starts.

As time passes and you add even more information and finish positions to your race-result charts, you should start to see patterns forming, and you will take note of the races in which several horses all came out and performed well in their next starts.

As you research past-performance lines of horses running today by going back to their prior charts, you will uncover much critical information and angles relevant to today's event. This is when you will surely recognize previous races as becoming key races by noting the finish positions of horses that have come out of these races.

On the following pages I list the natural progression of how to chart finishing positions from race to race so that you can easily spot quality races based on the number of horses that perform well in their next starts.

FIFTH RACE
Belmont
OCTOBER 12, 2001

6 FURLONGS. (1.07³) MAIDEN SPECIAL WEIGHT. Purse $41,000 (Up To $7,954 NYSBFOA) For Maiden Three Year Olds And Upward. Three Year Olds 118 lbs.; Older 121 lbs. (New york breds allowed 3 lbs.).

Value of Race: $41,000 Winner $24,600; second $8,200; third $4,510; fourth $2,460; fifth $1,230. Mutuel Pool $368,279.00 Exacta Pool $376,950.00 Trifecta Pool $286,934.00

Last Raced	Horse	M/Eqt. A.Wt	PP	St	¼	½	Str	Fin	Jockey	Odds $1
16Aug01 4Sar²	Cherokee Beau	L 3 118	6	6	5½	6⁸	2½	1½	Bailey J D	1.35
6Oct01 5Bel⁷	Mazaaham	Lf 4 121	7	5	4¹	1½	1½	2⁵	Velazquez J R	8.40
22Sep01 2Bel³	Rover	Lb 4 121	2	3	6ʰᵈ	4ʰᵈ	3½	3³½	Santos J A	4.70
22Sep01 2Bel⁵	B Of A Son	L 4 121	5	1	3¹	2ʰᵈ	4ʰᵈ	4¾	Arroyo N Jr	12.40
22Sep01 2Bel⁴	Fiercely	Lb 3 118	1	2	2ʰᵈ	5½	5²	5⁶½	Castellano J J	5.30
22Sep01 2Bel²	Turn Back The Time	Lbt 3 118	3	4	1ʰᵈ	3ʰᵈ	6¹²	6¹²½	Prado E S	3.65
6Nov98 1Med⁷	Keeto	t 5 114	4	7	7	7	7	7	Medina R Jr⁷	69.00

OFF AT 3:06 Start Good. Won driving. Track fast.
TIME :22⁴, :40⁰, :50⁴, 1:11¹ (:22.91, .40.50, .50.85, 1:11.39)

$2 Mutuel Prices:

6–CHEROKEE BEAU	4.70	3.40	2.40
7–MAZAAHAM		8.90	4.60
2–ROVER			3.50

$2 EXACTA 6–7 PAID $31.60 $2 TRIFECTA 6–7–2 PAID $116.50

Dk. b. or br. c, (May), by Cherokee Run–Beau Prospector, by Mr. Prospector. Trainer Alexander Frank A. Bred by J Mack Robinson (Ky).

CHEROKEE BEAU raced close up inside, split rivals in midstretch, finished gamely and prevailed under a drive. MAZAAHAM rallied four wide approaching the stretch and dug in gamely to the wire. ROVER was outrun early, put in a five wide run on the turn and faded in the final furlong. B OF A SON contested the pace while three wide and tired in the stretch. FIERCELY contested the pace along the inside and tired. TURN BACK THE TIME contested the pace while between rivals and tired. KEETO raced inside and tired.

Owners— 1, Robinson Jesse M; 2, Shadwell Stable; 3, Lazy F Ranch; 4, Anstu Stables; 5, Overbrook Farm; 6, Cotran Camille; 7, Quintina Worsfold

Trainers—1, Alexander Frank A; 2, Peitz Daniel C; 3, Penna Angel Jr; 4, Moloney James J; 5, Lukas D Wayne; 6, Imperio Leonard; 7, Worsfold Quintina

$2 Daily Double (7–6) Paid $8.60; Daily Double Pool $90,142.
$2 Pick Three (2–7–6) Paid $74.50; Pick Three Pool $65,368.

As illustrated, after breaking down the fractional times of the entire race, we then highlight the better parts of it. In this example, that means the first two quarters. We then highlight which horses were on the lead or very close to the early lead, since the better part of this race was the early portion.

The highlighted horses are Turn Back The Time, Fiercely, B Of A Son, and Mazaaham. Each was either on the lead or within about a length of the lead under the best fractions of the race, within the first half-mile.

The first horse to run back after exiting this race on October 12 was Fiercely. He was entered next on October 25, 2001, and finished 3rd. I then noted this finish position on the October 12 chart as illustrated below.

FIFTH RACE
Belmont
OCTOBER 12, 2001

6 FURLONGS. (1.073) MAIDEN SPECIAL WEIGHT. Purse $41,000 (Up To $7,954 NYSBFOA) For Maiden Three Year Olds And Upward. Three Year Olds 118 lbs.; Older 121 lbs. (New york breds allowed 3 lbs.).

Value of Race: $41,000 Winner $24,600; second $8,200; third $4,510; fourth $2,460; fifth $1,230. Mutuel Pool $368,279.00 Exacta Pool $376,950.00 Trifecta Pool $286,934.00

Last Raced	Horse	M/Eqt. A.Wt	PP	St	1/4	1/2	Str	Fin	Jockey	Odds $1
16Aug01 4Sar2	Cherokee Beau	L 3 118	6	6	5½	68	2½	1½	Bailey J D	1.35
5Oct01 5Bel7	Mazaaham	Lf 4 121	7	5	41	1½	1½	25	Velazquez J R	8.40
22Sep01 2Bel3	Rover	Lb 4 121	2	3	6hd	4hd	3½	33¼	Santos J A	4.70
22Sep01 2Bel5	B Of A Son	L 4 121	5	1	31	2hd	4hd	4¾	Arroyo N Jr	12.40
22Sep01 2Bel4	Fiercely	Lb 3 118	1	2	2hd	5½	52	56½	Castellano J J	5.30
22Sep01 2Bel2	Turn Back The Time	Lbf 3 118	3	4	1hd	3hd	612	612¼	Prado E S	3.65
6Nov98 1Med7	Keeto	f 5 114	4	7	7	7	7	7	Medina R Jr7	69.00

Since Fiercely came back to run third and the other horses highlighted on October 12 ran better races than he did, I now expect them to come back and run well. Of course I know I still have to handicap the races they will be entered in, but I feel I have an advantage because of this additional information.

The next horse to come out of the October 12 race was Turn Back The Time, on November 6. He won at odds of 2-1 and I noted his finish on the October 12 race chart, as I had done with Fiercely.

FIFTH RACE
Belmont
OCTOBER 12, 2001

6 FURLONGS. (1.07³) MAIDEN SPECIAL WEIGHT. Purse $41,000 (Up To $7,954 NYSBFOA) For Maiden Three Year Olds And Upward. Three Year Olds 118 lbs.; Older 121 lbs. (New york breds allowed 3 lbs.).

Value of Race: $41,000 Winner $24,600; second $8,200; third $4,510; fourth $2,460; fifth $1,230.   Mutuel Pool $368,279.00 Exacta Pool $376,950.00   Trifecta Pool $286,934.00

Last Raced	Horse	M/Eqt. A.Wt	PP St	¼	½	Str Fin	Jockey	Odds $1
16Aug01 4Sar²	Cherokee Beau	L 3 118	6 6	5½	6⁸	2½ 1½	Bailey J D	1.35
5Oct01 5Bel⁷	Mazaaham	Lf 4 121	7 5	4¹	1½	1½ 2⁵	Velazquez J R	8.40
22Sep01 2Bel³	Rover	Lb 4 121	2 3	6hd	4hd	3½ 33¼	Santos J A	4.70
22Sep01 2Bel⁵	B Of A Son	L 4 121	5 1	3¹	2hd	4hd 4¾	Arroyo N Jr	12.40
22Sep01 2Bel⁴	Fiercely	Lb 3 118	1 2	2hd	5½	5² 56½	Castellano J J	5.30
22Sep01 2Bel²	Turn Back The Time	Lbf 3 118	3 4	1hd	3hd	6¹² 6¹²¼	Prado E S	3.65
6Nov98 1Med⁷	Keeto	f 5 114	4 7	7	7	7 7	Medina R Jr⁷	69.00

Cherokee Beau was entered on November 8 and won at odds of 7-1. Although I did not highlight his effort on October 12th because he came from off the pace and didn't seem to be in contention during the better part of that race, his win following that effort just adds more depth and quality to an already key race.

The horse I am now watching for in the entries is B Of A Son. I originally highlighted his effort on October 12 as being solid, and now two horses he outran to the first half-mile have come out of the race to return with a win and a third-place finish, so it is natural to have some confidence that B Of A Son will also return with a huge effort in his next race.

In his following effort, on December 1, 2001, B Of A Son won at odds of 3-1.

SECOND RACE   6 FURLONGS. (1.07²) MAIDEN SPECIAL WEIGHT. Purse $41,000 (Up To $7,954 NYSBFOA) For Maiden Three Year Olds And Upward. Three Year Olds 120 lbs.; Older 121 lbs.

Aqueduct
DECEMBER 1, 2001

Value of Race: $41,000 Winner $24,600; second $8,200; third $4,510; fourth $2,460; fifth $1,230.   Mutuel Pool $276,046.00 Exacta Pool $284,744.00   Quinella Pool $35,298.00 Trifecta Pool $213,876.00

Last Raced	Horse	M/Eqt.	A.Wt	PP	St	$\frac{1}{4}$	$\frac{1}{2}$	Str	Fin	Jockey	Odds $1
12Oct01 5Bel⁴	B Of A Son	Lb	4 121	5	1	12½	1³	1⁶	12¾	Arroyo N Jr	3.85
6Nov01 1Aqu⁵	Freedom Onthe Wind	Lb	3 110	6	2	32½	25	24½	21½	Arroyo Nelson¹⁰	40.25
21Nov01 6Aqu⁴	Blazing Chief		5 116	4	7	6ʰᵈ	51	34½	34¼	Pimentel J⁵	6.10
18Nov01 4Aqu⁹	Protocol	L	3 120	1	6	55	68	52½	43½	Castellano J J	3.55
21May01 4Del⁶	Chief Scout	Lb	3 120	3	5	48	43½	4ʰᵈ	54	Bridgmohan S X	16.10
	Two Beat	L	3 120	7	4	7	7	7	6²	Migliore R	1.00
29Sep01 7Pha⁷	French Cat	L	3 115	2	3	2ʰᵈ	3ʰᵈ	66	7	Velazquez D C⁵	46.25

OFF AT 12:56 Start Good. Won driving. Track fast.
TIME :21³, :44⁴, :57¹, 1:10¹ (:21.76, :44.85, :57.24, 1:10.36)

$2 Mutuel Prices:

5–B OF A SON	9.70	5.20	4.40
6–FREEDOM ONTHE WIND		22.40	11.20
4–BLAZING CHIEF			3.40

$2 EXACTA 5–6 PAID $177.00 $2 QUINELLA 5–6 PAID $100.00 $2 TRIFECTA
5–6–4 PAID $702.00

B. c, by Deposit Ticket–Windago, by Hail the Pirates. Trainer Moloney James J. Bred by Hedgewood Farm (Ky).

B OF A SON quickly sprinted clear, set the pace and widened under a drive. FREEDOM ONTHE WIND chased the pace from the outside and held the place spot. BLAZING CHIEF raced inside and offered a mild rally on the rail. PROTOCOL had no response when roused. CHIEF SCOUT was outrun. TWO BEAT raced very greenly while wide. FRENCH CAT tired after showing brief speed.

Owners— 1, Anstu Stables; 2, Rodliff Paul & Avakian Stephen; 3, Andros Trish; 4, Siegel Samantha Mace & Jan; 5, Overbrook Farm; 6, Phipps Cynthia; 7, Singer Craig B

Trainers—1, Moloney James J; 2, Shannon Frank P; 3, Sherwood Colin; 4, Dutrow Richard E Jr; 5, Lukas D Wayne; 6, McGaughey Claude III; 7, Tesher Howard M

$2 Daily Double (4–5) Paid $88.00; Daily Double Pool $309,172.

This is an example of the basic train of thought and natural sequence to follow while charting horses' finish positions. Such record-keeping is time-consuming and occasionally a bit boring, but the groundwork will pay off down the road. It's an especially satisfying feeling when the horse coming out of a projected key race is going off at odds of 10-1 when you know he should be 2-1.

5

COMPARING
A DAY'S RACES

ANOTHER WAY OF projecting whether or not a particular race has a chance of turning into a key race is to try and determine its quality by comparing it to the rest of the races run on the same card.

The most convenient way to do this would be if you could match up identical races—ones run at the same distance and over the same surface, and at the same class—with the race you are trying to proof for quality. If that were possible, then it would be easy to make comparisons.

In reality, however, this is usually a rare occurrence, so further investigative work and critical thinking are needed to make thorough comparisons, and to determine just how good the race in question was.

The first step is to note the class of the races run on the card.

Obviously, if the race you are trying to proof was run at the highest class level on this day, then you want to see that it was the fastest event of the day. Or, if it wasn't the fastest in terms of final time, then perhaps most of the internal fractions were fastest.

On the other hand, if the race in question was not run at a higher class level than all the others on the card, then it doesn't necessarily need to be the fastest to still be considered a quality race. Instead, this race need only be almost as fast as the higher-class races to be deemed a good-quality effort.

The reason for this acceptable lower level of performance is that the race you are focusing on did not contain the classiest or best horses on the day, so you would not expect those horses to run the fastest times.

Further, while comparing race times, it is not essential that your race be the fastest at every fraction throughout. What you want to see is that your race was among the fastest for this day at a couple different fractional calls of time. This should enable you to declare a particular race to be a good-quality effort.

Let's suppose that you are researching a race chart in which a given horse was on the lead while putting up quick early fractions and weakened late. You want to try and find out just how quick, or how good, those fractions were in relation to the rest of the internal fractions posted during the day's other races. In order to verify that these early fractions were of a good quality, you need to compare them with the other early fractions.

If you compare the fractions in your race to those in one that was run at a lower class level, you need to see that your early fractions were faster. If you look at a race run at a higher class level, all you need to see is that, in the race in question, the fractions were just as fast; even if they are a tad slower, that would still be acceptable in most cases.

Further, if the fractions of the race you are trying to proof don't measure up to most of the races run this day, then take your analysis a step further and compare the final times. You don't want to leave a stone unturned when it comes to doing the investigative work to determine just how good or bad a race actually was.

The final time of a race is the product of the internal fractions, and it is easy to be fooled about the quality of an individual horse's performance based on a quick final time. In essence, however, it is not the final time that is most important, but how the final time was achieved.

For instance, if a horse came from the clouds and won a six-furlong race in 1:08 flat, the final time alone would be eye-catching. But the overall performance should not automatically be deemed better than the effort of a horse that dueled throughout the six furlongs under lightning-fast fractions and weakened late to finish in 1:10. Always remember that when you are comparing races on the same card—or, for that matter, any races run at the same distance—an understanding of how the final time was achieved is the most important aspect of the comparisons.

Race A = 1⅛ mile	46⅗	1:10	1:36	1:48
Race B = 1⅛ mile	48	1:11	1:36	1:47

In comparing these running lines, we see that Race A was run under quicker fractions while Race B has a faster final time. Although Race B has a faster finish, the effort given in Race A may be deemed to have more quality if the horse that won was on the lead earning these quicker fractions or was very close to these early splits.

There is an obvious difference in the early fractional splits of these two races. If a horse came from off the pace to win Race A, then he was running slower early fractions than those posted by the leader. Therefore, if the winning horse in Race A posted slower individual fractions en route to the final time of 1:48, then Race B might be the race with more quality, since the final time is faster. Of course, you also have to see how the final time in Race B was achieved.

With this in mind, it becomes clear that it is not the fractional or final time that is the most revealing aspect in trying to find quality within a running line; instead, it is the way these early fractions and final fractions are created.

Getting back to discussing comparisons of races on the same card, if the race you are examining does not compare favorably with the other races run the same day in terms of fractional and/or final times, then the next logical thing to do is wait and see how horses perform coming out of this race.

If we couldn't find an edge from the result charts, and didn't come up with an edge when we handicapped the race, we might as well be patient and wait to see how credibly this race shapes up, based on the performance of horses exiting this event.

As you go back into the charts and mark today's finish positions on these prior race charts on a daily basis, you will notice that more and more finish positions are filling in on the previous races. Therefore, the finish positions will help you determine the quality of any race in question.

Let's suppose that after comparing a certain race against the rest of the events on the card, the race in question stacks up favorably. This race now should be declared to be a projected key race.

The next step is to simply add these projected notes stating how the race matches up against the remainder of day's races. We would then highlight on the chart the part of the race that makes it better than the rest. We would highlight early fractions, final times, and the horses that earned these impressive notations.

At this point we have noted that the quality of this race is superior time-wise to that of the other races run on this same day. You are now laying excellent groundwork in regard to charting races, and when a horse is entered to run back out of this projected key race, this critical information is awaiting your research and analysis.

The next step regarding a projected key race could go in two directions. One option would be to wait and see how the first horse exiting this event performs in his next start. The other direction would be based on one's handicapping abilities. Since you always handicap a race before going to research your race-result charts, let's suppose that you select a horse in a given race to turn in a big effort today through your handicapping.

Then, while going into your race-result charts to research this horse's last race, you realize that he is coming out of a race you projected as being a possible key race. When I find that I have selected the same horse to run a big race today using two different methods—the first solely based on my handicapping skills, and the second method based on my race-result charts groundwork—it sends my confidence level through the roof!

In essence, if you put the groundwork into your race charts, your race charts will become very valuable. Doing the research, doing the daily comparisons, and highlighting the better than norm fractions and efforts will surely pay off in the long run.

6

TRIP NOTES AND
TRACK BIAS

*T*RIP NOTES ARE additional critical information that can be added to a race chart in order to help determine which horses might return with a big effort. They may indicate how a horse looks before the race, during the running, or even afterward.

While trip notes often point out that a horse experienced a tough trip and was blocked, steadied, or altered course during a race, they can also include comments such as "washy post parade" or "hard to pull up."

It is pivotal to determine if the difficulty in a horse's trip hindered him enough to truly compromise his best chance of winning. Once this degree of difficulty is determined, one can better assess how well he might have run without the troubled trip.

Perhaps the hardest aspect of deciding how to evaluate a troubled-trip note or comment is that you might not have actually seen the running of that particular race for yourself. Now you have to interpret what happened through the eyes and words of the chart callers.

Comments such as "slow start" and "off slowly" are signals to toss this race from being considered a negative aspect in a horse's past performances. Most of the time, a horse that gets off slowly does not recover to be a major factor in the race. This horse should be given the benefit of the doubt and declared to be just as sharp or as highly regarded as his prior races would allow. In addition, when I read comments such as "raced greenly" or "raced erratically," I will dismiss the effort.

Comments such as "checked," "steadied," "taken up," or "altered course" obviously can also mean that a horse was deprived of victory, but these should be assessed in a rational manner. Exactly where the horse encountered trouble might be the most telling element in determining just how serious the incident was, and to what degree it interfered with the performance.

For instance, the trouble might have occurred after the horse showed signs he was about to bow out of contention. Further, this horse might not have been in contention at all and might not have ever threatened or been a factor before this trouble occurred. In these cases, the trouble line can be misleading. However, if the horse that encountered trouble was in the midst of a rally or starting to gain on the leaders and was then faced with poor racing luck, the legitimacy of the trouble comments is magnified. How much leeway I allow for the lesser performance will depend on these circumstances.

Obviously it is preferable to watch as many races as possible at the racing circuits you follow. Along with trip handicapping, another advantage is getting the distinct sense of how each track surface is playing on a daily basis. This, of course, will aid in discovering if a bias of any kind exists.

A particular track condition can move a horse up or down against a given field. When considering the effect of moisture within a dirt-racing surface, for example, note that a track that is labeled wet-fast, good, or sloppy usually benefits the early-speed types. The opposite can be said for a muddy or heavy surface, where such conditions would favor a horse running from off the early pace.

By watching a previous day's races, one can get a better sense of exactly how the track was playing and in which direction it might be headed before the start of today's card. For instance, suppose it rained very heavily during the last three races on the prior day's card, and the official track condition went from fast to sloppy. For today's first race, however, the track condition is labeled fast.

In some instances a track will be called fast but will still have a certain amount of moisture within its surface. This is important to realize, since moisture tends to favor speed types; also, some horses do move up considerably on a wet surface. Of course, the best way to decide if there is moisture in a surface is to watch the horses as they enter the track before that first race. Are the horses kicking up a lot of loose dirt? Is the dirt sticking to their legs, chests, or underbellies? Is the dirt being kicked up or does it seem to be splattering? Are the outriders' horses wet?

Keep in mind that a racing surface can change in a very short time, even if it appears that the weather might not have changed at all. This is especially true with a track surface that started out wet and is drying out as the day goes on. In an attempt not to be at a disadvantage before an actual race is run, I always try and stay conscious of how a track was playing the previous race day before I handicap today's card.

In the course of doing my work, I will judge today's actual racing surface several times—before the start of today's races, during today's early races, and then again after the first few races have been assessed. This ensures that I am selecting horses that favor today's running conditions. It will also maintain the highest level of accuracy in reading how a track might play out the rest of the day and help me realize if a bias exists while I can still do something about it at the betting windows.

For instance, suppose the turf course seemed very hard on Tuesday and yielded quick early fractions as well as final times. The early-speed types seemed to last longer on the lead than they figured to, and there also was a gate-to-wire winner on the grass. Then say it rained overnight into Wednesday morning. The turf course now figures to be much softer, and will probably be labeled good or soft instead of the previous day's condition of firm. Since a grass course usually gets softer and slower when it gets wet during an overnight change in weather conditions, the speed types in the race might now be at a disadvantage, as opposed to the previous day.

To arrive at accurate conclusions one must ask certain questions about the racing surfaces. Did the speed horses hold up better than expected? Did any inside-speed horses last for the win? Did any horses gain any ground through the stretch? If so, what part of the track were they running on? Have the fractional times been dull? If so, when did it rain last? If the surface is dull, how have the early-speed types been holding up through the stretch?

Weather and surface notes should be added to the race-result charts for future reference so that an accurate assessment of the quality of today's races and efforts can be reached. The next time you look back to see the notes you created on a certain horse or race, you might be overjoyed to read this information. You might discover that on this particular day, a certain horse rallied through the teeth of an incredible speed bias to finish a nonthreatening third. While comparing this horse to the rest of today's field, you realize that he seems to fit better than most handicappers realize, and that his odds are higher than they should be.

Such record keeping will also help determine whether a particular horse might have run better than he figured to, thanks to that day's racing surface. Here again you have a huge edge. Such a horse will most likely take more money than he should at the windows today due to this surface-aided big effort, but you know that he is more vulnerable than his last race would indicate.

This kind of quality information added to a race chart cannot be found or purchased anywhere. It has to be created and recorded by a keen eye. Now you are investing with information you created.

7

RACE-DAY NOTES

ON THE FOLLOWING pages are a day's race-result charts with the notes I added while watching these races unfold. Included are trip notes, surface notes, and visual-performance notes. In sum, they are the account of what took place during the running of each race as I saw it.

I like to add my notes right onto my *Racing Form*. I do this to keep all my race information in one place until I can transfer it to my race charts. Whichever way you choose to list your race-day notes, the most important factor to remember is to make them as soon as possible after a race has been run. If you wait, it's all too easy to overlook or forget exactly what happened during each race. The original feeling you got from a given horse's performance will leave you once you have watched other races that followed on the card.

Another reason to take notes as each race unfolds is to be able to render a truer judgment of how the racing surface is playing. This is very important when trying to decipher if a bias existed and to what degree was it present. Making notes as each race unfolds will make it much easier to detect whether today's racing surface aided any horses.

Simply by keeping trip and surface notes you will be able to realize what actually happened on this day. You're going to be creating yet another edge for yourself because you will be investing with the use of information not too many handicappers will have.

Another reason to stay aware regarding the track condition is that a racing surface can change in minutes.

On April 26, 2002, at Aqueduct, the main track was labeled muddy and turf racing was canceled. I reasoned that horses running from off the pace might have an advantage in the early races as compared to the speed types, so I tried to find several horses in the early races that would best suit today's surface conditions.

I was also going to watch to see if any speed types held up better than expected and to learn if there was a bias toward either the inside or the outside. This is always important, since racetracks never dry out evenly.

The notes and comments on the day's charts below were created as the day went on.

Rained Heavily Prior Day

Surface aided win　　*Big effort -vs- grain*

RACE 1 Aqu–26Apr02 6 Furlongs(1.07²), 4↑ Clm 25000

Value of Race: $25,000. 1sts $10,000 each; 3rd $2,750; 4th $1,125 each. Mutuel Pools: $219,666, Ex $240,344

Last Raced	Horse	M/Eq	A	Wt	PP	St	¼	½	Str	Fin	Odds$1
10Apr02 4Aqu2 DH	Two Tour	Lb	5	120	3	3	3½	3hd	3⁵	1	2.80
7Apr02 9Aqu1 DH	Adams Gold Nugget	Lf	7	120	5	1	1¹½	1½	12½	1¾	1.85
10Apr02 9Aqu2	Above the Crowd	Lf	9	115	6	2	2½	2¹½	2hd	3⁸¾	4.40
10Apr02 4Aqu3 DH	Protist	Lb	5	120	1	5	4hd	5½	5½	4	a-2.35
11Jan02 2Aqu3 DH	Halo Flash	Lb	7	118	2	6	6	6	6	4nk	a-2.35
10Apr02 9Aqu9	Devil's Ransom	Lbf	7	120	4	4	5²½	4²½	4²	6	11.70

DH—Dead Heat.
a-Coupled: Protist and Halo Flash.

Very game

OFF 1:00 Start Good. Won driving. Track muddy.
TIME :22³, :45⁴, :58, 1:10³ (:22.66, :45.94, :58.01, 1:10.62)

3– DH TWO TOUR	3.50	3.50	2.80
6– DH ADAMS GOLD NUGGETT	3.10	3.60	2.70
7– ABOVE THE CROWD			2.60

$2 Ex (3-6) 11.60　　　　　　　　　　　　　$2 Ex (6-3) 10.60

Two Tour—D. g, by Tour d'Or Bebelu, by Buckaroo. Trainer Aquilino Joseph. Bred by James F Berry (Fla).

Adams Gold Nuggett—Gr/ro g, by Fountain of Gold–Adam's Run, by Fairway Phantom. Trainer Martin Frank. Bred by Adams Ann & John P (Fla).

TWO TOUR raced close up inside, responded when roused and finished gamely on the rail to dead heat for the win, driving. ADAMS GOLD NUGGETT quickly showed in front, set the pace and dug in gamely to finish on even terms for the win, driving. ABOVE THE CROWD raced with the pace from the outside and dug in gamely through the stretch. PROTIST had no rally. HALO FLASH raced wide and had no rally. DEVIL'S RANSOM chased three wide and tired.

Claiming prices—1, 25000; 2, 25000; 3, 25000; 4, 25000; 5, 22500; 6, 25000

Jockeys—1, Velazquez J R; 2, Gryder A T; 3, Galarza N; 4, Bridgmohan S X; 5, Arroyo N Jr; 6, Lopez C C

Trainers–1, Aquilino Joseph; 2, Martin Frank; 3, Lake Scott A; 4, Imperio Joseph; 5, Imperio Joseph; 6, Contessa Gary C

Owners—1, Dickstein Geoff; 2, Team Jomar Stable; 3, Lake Scott A; 4, Connolly Matthew B; 5, Roberts James K; 6, Moss Maggie

Two Tour was claimed by Gasper Gary; trainer, Lake Scott A.
Protist was claimed by Fathernson Stable; trainer, Barbara Robert.
Scratched— Electra Q Shun (28Mar02 8AQU5), Real American (10Apr02 4AQU8)

Surface seemed to be deep, which hurt speed types

RACE 2 Aqu–26Apr02 7 Furlongs(1.20), 4 ↑ Clm 20000

Value of Race: $21,000. 1st $12,600; 2nd $4,200; 3rd $2,310; 4th $1,260; 5th $630. Mutuel Pools: $156,284, Ex $194,449, Quin $21,598, DD $219,607

Last Raced	Horse	M/Eq	A	Wt	PP	St	¼	½	Str	Fin	Odds$1
7Apr02 ^{6}Aqu^{7}	Mickey The Groom	L	4	120	4	3	5	5	3^{3}	1^{hd}	2.70
7Apr02 ^{8}Pha^{8}	Luft	Lb	4	120	2	4	$4^{4\frac{1}{2}}$	$2\frac{1}{2}$	1^{hd}	$2^{1\frac{1}{4}}$	2.50
7Apr02 ^{9}Aqu^{6}	Carpe Demon	Lb	4	116	1	5	$1^{2\frac{1}{2}}$	$1\frac{1}{2}$	$2\frac{1}{2}$	$3^{5\frac{1}{4}}$	17.70
17Mar02 ^{5}Aqu^{1}	Mark's Mane Man	L	6	122	3	2	3^{hd}	$3\frac{1}{2}$	4^{20}	4^{23}	1.05
27Mar02 ^{4}Aqu^{6}	Private Cat	Lb	4	111	5	1	2^{hd}	$4^{3\frac{1}{2}}$	5	5	11.70

—Surface aided win
Good effort
Gamely

OFF 1:28 Start Good. Won driving. Track muddy.
TIME :23^{3}, :46^{4}, 1:11^{4}, 1:25 (:23.74, :46.87, 1:11.97, 1:25.03)

5–MICKEY THE GROOM	7.40	4.10	4.10
2–LUFT		4.10	3.60
1–CARPE DEMON			6.60

$2 Ex (5-2) 27.80 $2 Quin (2-5) 16.00 $2 DD (3-5) 16.80
$2 DD (6-5) 16.00

B. c, by Runaway Groom–Entire Order, by Broad Brush. Trainer Juvonen Erik. Bred by Brereton C Jones (Ky).

MICKEY THE GROOM was outrun early, rallied four wide approaching the stretch, dug in determinedly and was along late from the outside, driving. LUFT raced with the pace while between rivals and dug in gamely through the stretch. CARPE DEMON set the pace along the inside and continued on stubbornly in the stretch. MARK'S MANE MAN chased the pace while three wide and tired. PRIVATE CAT chased the pace while four wide and tired.

Claiming prices—1, 20000; 2, 20000; 3, 18000; 4, 20000; 5, 18000

Jockeys— 1, Arroyo N Jr; 2, Gryder A T; 3, Pezua J M; 4, Prado E S; 5, Villafan R

Trainers– 1, Juvonen Erik; 2, Imperio Joseph; 3, Moschera Gasper S; 4, Klesaris Robert P; 5, Araya Rene A

Owners— 1, Gambone Michael; 2, Imperio Joseph; 3, Davis Barbara J; 4, Bada Bing Stable; 5, Petronella Robert A

Mark's Mane Man was claimed by Goldfarb Sanford J; trainer, Dutrow Richard E Jr.

Scratched— Foxy Beau (29Mar02 ^{2}AQU^{2})

Still favoring closers

RACE 3 Aqu–26Apr02 7 Furlongs(1.20), 4 ↑ Ⓕ Clm 35000

Value of Race: $31,500. 1st $18,900; 2nd $6,300; 3rd $3,465; 4th $1,890; 5th $945. Mutuel Pools: $292,628, Ex $283,021, Tri $177,665

Last Raced	Horse	M/Eq	A	Wt	PP	St	¼	½	Str	Fin	Odds$1
12Apr02 ^{3}Aqu^{1}	Nikita	Lf	7	123	2	6	$2\frac{1}{2}$	$2^{1\frac{1}{2}}$	1^{hd}	1^{hd}	3.05
22Mar02 ^{4}Aqu^{1}	Won Moro	Lf	5	122	5	2	$3\frac{1}{2}$	$3^{1\frac{1}{2}}$	$2^{2\frac{1}{2}}$	2^{4}	2.50
12Apr02 ^{3}Aqu^{2}	Pro Motion Days	Lbf	6	117	4	4	4^{hd}	4^{hd}	3^{hd}	3^{hd}	4.40
4Apr02 ^{3}Aqu^{1}	Brightest	Lb	5	120	3	7	5^{2}	5^{7}	4^{3}	4^{5}	6.90
12Apr02 ^{6}Aqu^{5}	Sign Of Courage	Lbf	6	118	1	5	7	7	6^{2}	$5^{2\frac{1}{4}}$	12.30
7Apr02 ^{4}Aqu^{3}	Lavish	Lf	4	120	7	1	$1\frac{1}{2}$	1^{hd}	$5^{3\frac{1}{2}}$	$6^{3\frac{1}{2}}$	7.10
4Apr02 ^{4}GP^{7}	Lorraine	L	5	120	6	3	6^{1}	$6\frac{1}{2}$	7	7	7.00

—Got away with very slow fractions

OFF 1:56 Start Good. Won driving. Track good.
TIME :23^{3}, :47^{1}, 1:12^{3}, 1:25^{1} (:23.66, :47.28, 1:12.67, 1:25.34)

2–NIKITA	8.10	3.90	2.80
5–WON MORO		3.90	2.60
4–PRO MOTION DAYS			2.80

$2 Ex (2-5) 25.80 $2 Tri (2-5-4) 87.00

Dk. b. or br. m, by Slew City Slew–Threat of Peace, by Hold Your Peace. Trainer Klesaris Robert P. Bred by Haras du Chevrillard (Que–C).

NIKITA contested the pace along the inside, dug in resolutely in the stretch and prevailed after a long drive. WON MORO raced close up outside, rallied three wide nearing the stretch and battled gamely to the wire. PRO MOTION DAYS raced close up while four wide and lacked a rally. BRIGHTEST raced close up inside and had no rally. SIGN OF COURAGE raced inside and had no response when roused. LAVISH set the pace while between rivals and tired in the stretch. LORRAINE had no rally.

Claiming prices—1, 35000; 2, 35000; 3, 35000; 4, 30000; 5, 30000; 6, 35000; 7, 35000

Jockeys— 1, Prado E S; 2, Luzzi M J; 3, Lopez C C; 4, Bridgmohan S X; 5, Gryder A T; 6, Santos J A; 7, Davis R G

Trainers– 1, Klesaris Robert P; 2, Levine Bruce N; 3, Imperio Joseph; 4, Ramos Faustino F; 5, Friedman Mitchell; 6, Galluscio Dominic G; 7, Hough Stanley M

Owners— 1, C D & G Stable; 2, Baron Robert J; 3, Our Metro Stable & Montilli Tony; 4, Ramos Faustino F; 5, Parra Rosendo G; 6, Ball John D Paris Raymond & Karr Ro; 7, Stanley M Hough & John Pastorek

Nikita was claimed by Goldfarb Sanford J; trainer, Dutrow Richard E Jr.
Won Moro was claimed by Bada Bing Stable; trainer, Klesaris Robert P.
Lavish was claimed by Schosberg Dawn; trainer, Schosberg Richard.

Surface upgraded to Good

RACE 4 Aqu–26Apr02 1 Mile⊗(1.32^{2}), 3↑ Alw 46000n2x S

Value of Race: \$46,000. 1st \$27,600; 2nd \$9,200; 3rd \$5,060; 4th \$2,760; 5th \$1,380. Mutuel Pools: \$215,274, Ex \$310,327, Quin \$35,786, Tri \$215,191, Pick–3 \$60,770

Last Raced	Horse	M/Eq	A	Wt	PP	St	¼	½	¾	Str	Fin	Odds\$1
30Mar02 ^{7}Aqu^{8}	Go Big Blue	Lb	4	122	12	3	11^{3}	$8^{\frac{1}{2}}$	$3^{\frac{1}{2}}$	$1^{3\frac{1}{2}}$	$1^{4\frac{1}{4}}$	7.10
6Apr02 ^{13}GP^{5}	Saf Link	L	4	122	8	4	4^{hd}	6^{hd}	$4^{1\frac{1}{2}}$	2^{2}	$2^{2\frac{1}{4}}$	4.00
12Apr02 ^{1}Aqu^{1}	Dudini Houdini	Lb	4	122	9	10	10^{hd}	$9^{\frac{1}{2}}$	$6^{1\frac{1}{2}}$	4^{hd}	$3^{2\frac{1}{2}}$	a-8.00
30Mar02 ^{7}Aqu^{6}	Lilt	Lb	3	114	4	9	5^{hd}	4^{hd}	5^{2}	5^{2}	4no	6.30
15Mar02 ^{4}GP^{2}	Ham Sandwich	L	5	122	6	12	12	12	8^{2}	6^{hd}	5^{2}	6.00
17Apr02 ^{7}Aqu^{4}	Graceful Devil	Lbf	4	122	7	8	9^{hd}	$7^{\frac{1}{2}}$	7^{hd}	8^{3}	$6^{\frac{3}{4}}$	18.60
5Apr02 ^{7}Aqu^{5}	Online Intime	Lbf	6	122	11	2	$3^{1\frac{1}{2}}$	3^{hd}	2^{hd}	$3^{\frac{1}{2}}$	7^{5}	13.90
5Apr02 ^{7}Aqu^{4}	Anties Boy	Lbf	5	124	5	6	$2^{1\frac{1}{2}}$	2^{1}	1^{hd}	7^{hd}	8^{1}	a-8.00
21Jan02 ^{9}Aqu^{9}	On The Fan	L	5	122	10	1	$6^{1\frac{1}{2}}$	10^{3}	9^{2}	$9^{2\frac{1}{2}}$	9^{1}	58.50
11Apr02 ^{4}Aqu^{1}	Lake Marion	Lb	5	124	1	11	7^{hd}	5^{1}	10^{hd}	10^{2}	$10^{2\frac{1}{2}}$	25.00
16Feb02 ^{2}Aqu^{5}	No White Flags	L	4	122	2	7	8^{hd}	11^{hd}	12	$11^{5\frac{1}{2}}$	$11^{9\frac{3}{4}}$	20.10
13Apr02 ^{3}Aqu^{4}	Captain Nicholas	Lb	4	122	3	5	1^{hd}	$1^{\frac{1}{2}}$	11^{hd}	12	12	3.20

Full of Run - Loved the surface striding out nicely (Go Big Blue)

Mid Move but tired (Online Intime)

Tired Badly (Captain Nicholas)

a-Coupled: Dudini Houdini and Anties Boy.

OFF 2:25 Start Good. Won driving. Track good.

TIME :23^{2}, :46^{4}, 1:13^{1}, 1:38^{3} (:23.40, :46.93, 1:13.22, 1:38.66)

14–GO BIG BLUE	**16.20**	**6.80**	**4.20**
11–SAF LINK		**5.90**	**4.60**
1A–DUDINI HOUDINI (a-entry)			**4.90**

\$2 Ex (14-11) 79.00 \$2 Quin (11-14) 37.80 \$2 Tri (14-11-1) 568.00

\$2 Pick-3 (5-2-14) 202.00

Dk. b. or br. g, by Cure the Blues–Midnight Goer, by Two Punch. Trainer Donk David. Bred by Milfer Farm Inc P C Bance & J D Stuart (NY).

GO BIG BLUE was outrun early, rallied five wide on the turn and drew away under a drive. SAF LINK raced close up outside, rallied four wide on the turn, was no match for the winner but continued on to best the others. DUDINI HOUDINI was outrun early, raced four wide and lacked a rally. LILT raced close up while between rivals and had no rally. HAM SANDWICH was outrun early, put in a five wide run on the turn and had nothing left for the stretch drive. GRACEFUL DEVIL had no response when roused. ONLINE INTIME chased the pace while three wide and tired in the stretch. ANTIES BOY contested the pace along the inside and tired. ON THE FAN raced inside and tired. LAKE MARION tired after showing brief speed. NO WHITE FLAGS was outrun. CAPTAIN NICHOLAS showed speed for a half mile and tired.

Track Drying out seemed to be getting quicker

Jockeys— 1, Bridgmohan S X; 2, Prado E S; 3, Pimentel J; 4, Luzzi M J; 5, Santos J A; 6, Gryder A T; 7, Arroyo N Jr; 8, Samyn J L; 9, Migliore R; 10, Henry Wesley; 11, Davis R G; 12, Velazquez J R

Trainers– 1, Donk David; 2, Penna Angel Jr; 3, Ferraro James W; 4, Levine Bruce N; 5, Schulhofer Randy; 6, Friedman Mitchell; 7, Destefano John M Jr; 8, Ferraro James W; 9, Hertler John O; 10, Pringle Edmund; 11, Destasio Richard A; 12, Nevin Michael

Owners— 1, Marquis Charles K & Behrendt John T; 2, Santangelo Francis R; 3, Rudina Stable; 4, E El R Stable; 5, Leveen Leonard; 6, Sunny Meadow Farm; 7, Wachtel Edwin H; 8, Ferraro James W; 9, Summer Wind Stable; 10, Carney Elvis & Renardo & Pringle Ed; 11, Larkin Donald R Montilli Tony Toome; 12, O'Reilly Patricia & Panathenian Sta

Scratched— Appleturnover Mike (13Apr02 ^{3}AQU^{3}), Distant Dibo (19Apr02 ^{7}AQU^{7}), Robbie's Rockin (12Apr02 ^{8}AQU^{1}), Son (7Apr02 ^{9}AQU^{3})

RACE 5 Aqu–26Apr02 7 Furlongs(1.20), 3 ↑ Md Sp Wt

Value of Race: $41,000. 1st $24,600; 2nd $8,200; 3rd $4,510; 4th $2,460; 5th $1,230. Mutuel Pools: $335,848, Ex $321,190, Tri $213,697, Pick–3 $56,499

Last Raced	Horse	M/Eq	A	Wt	PP	St	1/4	1/2	Str	Fin	Odds$1
13Apr02 1Aqu2	Lucky Devil	Lb	4	123	5	1	25	26	17	17	0.90
	Global Quest		3	115	7	2	612	612	4hd	26¼	5.00
2Feb02 7GP3	Key Moment	L	4	123	1	3	11½	1½	23½	31¾	10.40
30Mar02 8GP6	Realist	Lb	3	115	4	6	51	45½	58	45	17.50
29Mar02 5Aqu4	Pull Over Please	f	3	115	2	7	35	33½	3½	55¾	2.75
	Polympics	L	3	115	3	5	4½	51	610	68	51.50
	South Of Dixie	L	3	115	6	4	7	7	7	7	16.50

OFF 2:53 Start Good. Won driving. Track good.
TIME :222, :453, 1:11, 1:243 (:22.48, :45.66, 1:11.06, 1:24.61)

5–LUCKY DEVIL	3.80	2.60	2.20
7–GLOBAL QUEST		3.80	2.70
1–KEY MOMENT			3.10

$2 Ex (5–7) 15.20 $2 Tri (5–7–1) 52.50 $2 Pick–3 (2–14–5) 186.00

B. c, by Devil's Bag–Quick Blush, by Blushing Groom*Fr. Trainer Jerkens James A. Bred by Kinghaven Farms Limited (Ont–C).

LUCKY DEVIL showed good speed from the outside while in hand, took over after the opening half mile and drew away under a drive. GLOBAL QUEST dropped back early while racing greenly, came wide into the stretch and was going well outside late. KEY MOMENT set the pace along the inside and tired in the stretch. REALIST had no rally. PULL OVER PLEASE chased the pace along the inside and tired in the stretch. POLYMPICS was outrun. SOUTH OF DIXIE raced very greenly.

Jockeys– 1, Gryder A T; 2, Velazquez J R; 3, Migliore R; 4, Arroyo N Jr; 5, Luzzi M J; 6, Castillo H Jr; 7, Prado E S

Trainers– 1, Jerkens James A; 2, McGaughey Claude III; 3, Mott William I; 4, Clement Christophe; 5, Levine Bruce N; 6, Schettino Dominick A; 7, Zito Nicholas P

Owners– 1, Stronach Stable; 2, Ogden Mills Phipps & William Acquav; 3, Wygod Mr & Mrs Martin J; 4, Karches Peter F & Harris Charles E; 5, Lickle William C; 6, Jester Michael W; 7, Marylou Whitney Stable

— Easily - Full of run

Broke well

Dropped back, Good finish

Surface getting quicker - No longer favoring closers

RACE 6 Aqu–26Apr02 6½ Furlongs(1.141), 4 ↑ Ⓕ Alw 47000n3x

Value of Race: $47,000. 1st $28,200; 2nd $9,400; 3rd $5,170; 4th $2,820; 5th $1,410. Mutuel Pools: $312,523, Ex $322,376, Pick–3 $47,863

Last Raced	Horse	M/Eq	A	Wt	PP	St	1/4	1/2	Str	Fin	Odds$1
3Apr02 8Aqu3	Home On The Hill	Lb	5	109	3	1	12	13½	15	11½	3.35
8Mar02 7GP2	Laurie's Balada	L	4	117	1	4	31½	2hd	21	2hd	2.40
10Apr02 5Aqu1	Favorite Ending	Lb	5	122	2	3	5	5	3½	3¾	12.40
7Apr02 8Aqu1	We'll Sea Ya	L	4	119	4	5	4½	42	4½	43	1.65
28Mar02 7Aqu1	Saskya	Lbf	4	122	5	2	2hd	31½	5	5	4.20

OFF 3:22 Start Good. Won driving. Track good.
TIME :23, :46, 1:111, 1:174 (:23.03, :46.12, 1:11.28, 1:17.98)

3–HOME ON THE HILL	8.70	4.20	2.60
1–LAURIE'S BALADA		4.00	3.20
2–FAVORITE ENDING			3.90

$2 Ex (3–1) 32.60 $2 Pick–3 (14–5–3) 129.50

B. m, by Scarlet Ibis–Dancing Incognito, by Masked Dancer. Trainer Mattis Errol. Bred by Ju–Ju–Gen Stables Inc (NY).

HOME ON THE HILL came away in good order and soon established a clear lead, made the pace while in hand, took a long lead into deep stretch and remained safely clear under a drive. LAURIE'S BALADA raced close up inside while in hand, came wide into the stretch and finished gamely outside to get the place spot. FAVORITE ENDING was outrun early, raced inside and finished well on the rail. WE'LL SEA YA raced wide and posed no real threat. SASKYA raced close up outside while in hand and tired.

Jockeys– 1, Villafan R; 2, Arroyo N Jr; 3, Davis R G; 4, Leon F; 5, Toscano P R

Trainers– 1, Mattis Errol; 2, Zito Nicholas P; 3, Moschera Gasper S; 4, Iorio Sal Jr; 5, Bush Thomas M

Owners– 1, Riley Gladstone A; 2, Hunt Nelson B; 3, Marinos Jane E & Alex A; 4, Iorio Carmine; 5, Berkshire Stud & Oak Cliff Stable

— Track carried her home

Good Finish

Had nothing

Speed Bias Now exists

RACE 7 Aqu–26Apr02 6 Furlongs(1.07²), 3 ↑ Alw 43000n1x

Value of Race: $43,000. 1st $25,800; 2nd $8,600; 3rd $4,730; 4th $2,580; 5th $1,290. Mutuel Pools: $391,139, Ex $357,845, Tri $261,994, DD $91,537, Pick–3 $59,431

Last Raced	Horse	M/Eq	A	Wt	PP	St	¼	½	Str	Fin	Odds$1
4Apr02 ⁸Aqu⁵	Gold Shark	Lb	4	118	8	1	1¹¹⁄₂	13½	1⁵	1¹¹⁄₄	5.10
19Apr02 ⁷Aqu¹	Magic And Bird	L	4	117	1	8	7¹¹⁄₂	4ʰᵈ	2³	2⁵³⁄₄	3.35
2Mar02 ⁷GP¹	Quantis	L	3	113	6	5	2¹	2½	3²	3¹¹⁄₄	1.70
13Oct01 ⁷Med⁵	H. M. S. Jackson	Lb	5	118	2	3	5½	5²½	4³	4³³⁄₄	5.10
24Mar02 ⁴GP³	Trumpster	Lb	5	118	4	7	6⁶	6ʰᵈ	5ʰᵈ	5²³⁄₄	11.90
13Apr02 ²Aqu⁵	Strike The Brass	L	5	117	7	4	3ʰᵈ	7¹⁰	7¹²	6⁴	11.50
14Apr02 ⁷Aqu⁹	Nashville Cat	Lb	4	113	5	6	4½	3²	6ʰᵈ	7⁹³⁄₄	17.50
16Mar02 ⁷Aqu⁵	Power Choice	Lbf	4	110	3	2	8	8	8	8	30.25

OFF 3:52 Start Good. Won driving. Track good.
TIME :22¹, :45⁴, :58, 1:10⁴ (:22.39, :45.89, :58.09, 1:10.86)

11–GOLD SHARK	12.20	6.00	3.40
1–MAGIC AND BIRD		4.70	2.90
7–QUANTIS			2.60

$2 Ex (11–1) 63.50 $2 Tri (11-1-7) 170.00 $2 DD (3–11) 47.00
$2 Pick–3 (5-3-11) 101.00

Ch. c, by Holy Bull–Fleet Wahine, by Afleet. Trainer Jerkens James A. Bred by Adena Springs (Ky).

GOLD SHARK was hustled out to a clear lead, set the pace, opened up turning for home then dug in and remained clear under a drive. MAGIC AND BIRD was outrun early, rallied inside on the turn, angled out in the stretch and finished gamely. QUANTIS was bumped at the start, chased the pace for a half mile and tired. H. M. S. JACKSON had no rally. TRUMPSTER was bumped after the start, raced four wide and tired. STRIKE THE BRASS was bumped at the start, chased the pace while three wide and tired. NASHVILLE CAT was bumped at the start, was steadied in tight quarters after the start, was rushed up three wide, chased the pace and tired. POWER CHOICE was outrun.

Jockeys— 1, Gryder A T; 2, Arroyo N Jr; 3, Prado E S; 4, Bravo J; 5, Velazquez J R; 6, Santos J A; 7, Villafan R; 8, Galarza N

Trainers– 1, Jerkens James A; 2, Aquilino Joseph; 3, Bond Harold James; 4, Hills Timothy A; 5, Alexander Frank A, 6, Odintz Jeff, 7, Jerkens H Allen, 8, Sedlacek Michael C

Owners— 1, Stronach Stable; 2, Paraneck Stable; 3, West Gary L & Mary E; 4, Rudolph Depolo Richard A Filosa & T; 5, Robinson Jesse M; 6, Karakorum Farm; 7, Cowan Marjorie & Irving M; 8, Rising Graph Stable

Scratched— Dynamic Lord (22Mar02 ⁷AQU³), Casual Country (12Apr02 ⁸AQU⁴), Poppy M (10Jan02 ⁵AQU⁸), Turn Back The Time (4Apr02 ⁸AQU²)

—Uncontested lead

Finished well against bias

Broke poorly, Rushed Lost all chance

RACE 8 Aqu–26Apr02 6 Furlongs(1.07²), 4↑ Alw 54000r

Value of Race: $54,000. 1st $32,400; 2nd $10,800; 3rd $5,940; 4th $3,240; 5th $1,620. Mutuel Pools: $304,853, Ex $381,021, Tri $185,405, Pick–6 $52,550 Carryover $31,530

Last Raced	Horse	M/Eq	A	Wt	PP	St	¼	½	Str	Fin	Odds$1
27Mar02 8Aqu²	Marshall Greeley	L	5	116	3	2	1hd	3hd	11	1¾	6.40
27Mar02 8Aqu¹	Late Carson	L	6	123	1	6	5²½	5hd	3½	2¹½	0.50
7Jun01 5Bel¹	Nevada Strip	L	5	116	2	4	4hd	4¹½	2¹½	3⁵½	7.00
9Nov01 8Med⁹	Oro de Mexico	L	8	118	6	1	2½	2hd	4hd	4¾	22.90
12May01 7Bel⁷	Chasin' Wimmin	L	7	113	4	5	6	6	6	5½	30.50
19Oct01 6Med⁷	Max's Pal	L	5	118	5	3	3½	1hd	5²	6	4.40

Handwritten notes: Surface Aided Win / Blocked badly Turn and Stretch - lost all chance / Needed the race

OFF 4:22 Start Good. Won driving. Track good.
TIME :22³, :46², :58², 1:10³ (:22.66, :46.43, :58.43, 1:10.60).

3–MARSHALL GREELEY	14.80	3.90	2.30
1–LATE CARSON		2.30	2.10
2–NEVADA STRIP			2.30

$2 Ex (3–1) 24.80 $2 Tri (3–1–2) 64.00
$2 Pick–6 (2–14–5–3–11–3) 5 Correct 2,627.00

Ch. h, by Mr. Greeley–She's Sofine, by Bold Hour. Trainer Juvonen Erik. Bred by C L Kidder Jeffrey Morris N Robenalt & G Comer (Ky).

MARSHALL GREELEY contested the pace along the inside, drew clear when roused in upper stretch then dug in gamely and held on, driving. LATE CARSON was steadied along on the rail, was blocked on the turn and again in upper stretch, was steadied again, altered course to the outside and finished gamely, too late. NEVADA STRIP raced close up outside, out in a four wide run approaching the stretch and continued on gamely to the finish. ORO DE MEXICO contested the pace while three wide and tired in the final furlong. CHASIN' WIMMIN raced wide throughout and had no rally. MAX'S PAL contested the pace while between rivals and tired in the stretch.

Jockeys— 1, Bridgmohan S X; 2, Velazquez J R; 3, Luzzi M J; 4, Lopez C C; 5, Samyn J L; 6, Bravo J

Trainers— 1, Juvonen Erik; 2, Dutrow Richard E Jr; 3, Levine Bruce N; 4, Serpe Philip M; 5, Hertler John O; 6, Perkins Ben W Jr

Owners— 1, Gambone Michael; 2, Goldfarb Sanford Belnap Tyler & Ros; 3, Lickle William C; 4, John T Dee & Thomas Moran; 5, Cohn Seymour; 6, Dweck Raymond

RACE 9 Aqu–26Apr02 6 Furlongs(1.07^{2}), 3↑ Md Sp Wt S

Value of Race: $41,000. 1st $24,600; 2nd $8,200; 3rd $4,510; 4th $2,460; 5th $1,230. Mutuel Pools: $390,414, Ex $370,068, Tri $300,046, Super $127,547, DD $228,866, Pick–3 $88,050, Pick–4 $158,399

Last Raced	Horse	M/Eq	A	Wt	PP	St	¼	½	Str	Fin	Odds$1
	Be That Way	Lf	3	115	7	8	6^{hd}	4^{3}	1½	16¼	8.90
6Apr02 ^{5}Aqu^{3}	Aeras	Lb	3	115	2	5	1½	22½	2^{1}	21¾	4.80
	Exceptional Gift		4	123	5	3	7^{1}	5½	4^{5}	31½	10.70
11Apr02 ^{9}Aqu^{4}	Hey Brother	Lb	3	115	3	2	2½	1^{hd}	34½	43¼	1.80
10Mar02 ^{3}Aqu^{8}	Captain Tim	Lb	3	115	4	7	8	8	6½	54¾	3.00
20Apr02 ^{9}Aqu^{8}	Tamusky	Lbf	3	110	1	4	41½	72½	73½	6^{5}	93.75
11Apr02 ^{9}Aqu^{5}	A. P. Junior	L	3	115	8	1	3^{1}	31½	5^{1}	71¼	6.10
11Apr02 ^{9}Aqu^{7}	Karakorums R Wild	Lb	3	115	6	6	53½	6^{hd}	8	8	18.00

—Off slow, Full of Run (Be That Way)

Dropped back early, Finished well (Exceptional Gift)

OFF 4:51 Start Good. Won ridden out. Track good.
TIME :22^{2}, :46^{3}, :59^{4}, 1:12^{4} (:22.41, :46.68, :59.91, 1:12.88)

10–BE THAT WAY	19.80	8.60	6.70
3–AERAS		5.80	5.00
7–EXCEPTIONAL GIFT			5.40

$2 Ex (10-3) 97.00 $2 Tri (10-3-7) 665.00 $2 Super (10-3-7-4) 2,057.00
$2 DD (3-10) 149.00 $2 Pick-3 (11-3-10) 1,109.00 $2 Pick-4 (3-11-3-10) 3,599.00

Gr/ro c, (Apr), by Cryptoclearance–Last Two States, by Alaskan Frost. Trainer Hushion Michael E. Bred by Stonewall Farm (NY).

BE THAT WAY ducked out at the start, was outrun early, rallied inside on the turn, came wide into the stretch, ran by the leaders in midstretch and drew away, ridden out. AERAS was bumped at the start, contested the pace along the inside and continued on to hold the place. EXCEPTIONAL GIFT raced greenly along the inside early, angled out in the stretch and offered a mild rally outside. HEY BROTHER was bumped at the start, contested the pace from the outside and tired in the stretch. CAPTAIN TIM had no rally. TAMUSKY was bumped at the start, chased the pace along the inside and tired. A. P. JUNIOR chased the pace from the outside and tired in the stretch. KARAKORUMS R WILD raced wide and tired.

Jockeys— 1, Davis R G; 2, Bridgmohan S X; 3, Samyn J L; 4, Migliore R; 5, Velazquez J R; 6, Galarza N; 7, Rojas R I; 8, Santos J A

Trainers– 1, Hushion Michael E; 2, Klesaris Robert P; 3, Allard Edward T; 4, Doctofano John M Jr; 5, Schosberg Richard; 6, Cameron Raymond A; 7, Streicher Kenneth; 8, Odintz Jeff

Owners— 1, Schwartz Barry K; 2, G Lack Farms; 3, Blue Streak Stable; 4, Jujugen Stable; 5, Ryan Michael J; 6, Cameron Raymond A; 7, L I Brookline Stables; 8, Karakorum Farm

Scratched— Stimson House (31Jan02 ^{3}AQU^{7}), J. P.'s Amanda (6Apr02 ^{5}AQU^{4}), Storm City

Track Dried out as day went on and was favoring speed for last few races on day.

Aqueduct Attendance: 3,503 Mutuel Pool: $740,368.00 ITW Mutuel Pool: $2,585,799.00 ISW Mutuel Pool: $4,675,606.00

Now think how important these race-day notes and comments could be the next time you research a race or a horse that ran on this day. Obviously none of us can watch every race, but these notes illustrate why I try to focus on the weather and how the track has been playing by examining the charts of the races I miss.

8

POST POSITION
AND TURNS

POST POSITION CAN easily decide the outcome of any race before it even starts. Certain post positions for specific distances win so infrequently that, to my mind, a horse with such a poor post might have to be twice as good this day to beat a lesser horse with an advantageous post.

Take a look at the illustration below of a track diagram. This is the diagram of Belmont Park's inner turf course for a race run at 1 $\frac{1}{16}$ miles.

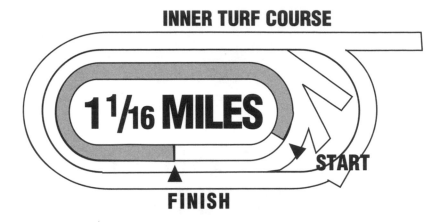

INNER TURF COURSE

Note that the race starts on a turn, which means that horses breaking from the outer posts will be at a huge disadvantage. They will have to use more energy out of the gate to establish a favorable running position, while the horses drawn to their inside might already be reserving their energy for the stretch run. If the horses in the outermost posts aren't hustled from the gate, they will simply have more to do to catch up.

There are specific distances and configurations at almost every racetrack where the percentages of winning will decrease as the post positions get wider. *Daily Racing Form* publishes regularly updated lists of winning post positions, and by being aware of these statistics, you can turn this situation into an edge.

Here again is a reason why understanding pace and being able to pace-rate a given field has its advantages. Through careful pace analysis, one can actually visualize where each horse will be positioned during the early stages of a race. With this in mind, it is very possible to get a good idea of just how much energy each horse will have to expend in order to attain an early tactical running position. This becomes even more important when trying to consider a horse's chances while breaking from the wider post positions.

Let's use the same diagram for Belmont Park at 1 $\frac{1}{16}$ miles on the inner turf to help understand the following example of a race scenario.

If an early-speed type is breaking from the widest post (in this case, post 10) and there are no other true speed types to his inside, one can assume that he will not have to use too much energy to break on top. His rider will then try to angle toward the inside as much as possible, darting over to the rail.

In this scenario, the horse that breaks from post 10 might not be at as much of a disadvantage as first thought. However, projecting what this horse might do in this situation is one thing, and knowing whether he has the ability to do it is another. By being able to judge this horse's rate of speed and whether he will be able to outbreak the horses to his inside, the well-informed handicapper has a big advantage.

Let's take this example a step in the other direction and say that the inside posts in this race contain truer early-speed types than the wider posts. If this is the case, the horses on the outside will be stuck wide going around that first turn whether they have any early speed or not. The horses starting from the wider posts will not be able to break on top and tuck in until the inner early speeds have already cleared that first turn. Therefore, these horses will quickly lose valuable ground and will find themselves out of the early running, playing catch-up for the rest of the race.

Of course, in each of these examples, one would have to assess which horses have the sharpest turn of early speed. The most important aspect of each and every race scenario is having the ability to visualize the likely pace setup and being able to accurately determine where each horse should be positioned as the race unfolds; this creates a huge edge.

This edge can be further realized by deciphering if a horse's post-position draw creates as big an advantage or disadvantage as first considered. As shown through the previous race examples, sometimes a horse's post position is not as clearly good or bad as you might first think before analyzing the pace abilities of the rest of today's field.

To turn post-position draws into an advantage with regard to how quickly that first turn comes up in relation to the starting-gate placement, one should know exactly where the starting gate is situated in relation to that first turn. Not all wide posts are considered poor starting positions. In fact, sometimes breaking from the rail post can be worse.

In charting races with regard to post positions, it is always wise to note which horses broke from disadvantageous positions for today's race. Considering this, a horse needn't win to earn high ratings if he broke from a terrible post and still went on to run a creditable race. In judging that performance, just how much leeway should be allowed? Well, that all depends on the set of circumstances within each race and the quality of the opposition. But by taking note of such information, you will turn your race-result charts into an invaluable handicapping tool. Usually a horse that had a poor post position last time out and ran a fair race for that reason will be overlooked in the betting next time out.

9

ADDITIONAL ANGLING

IN THE FOLLOWING chart, the best part of the race was the first three quarters of a mile. The fractional breakdowns were 22$\frac{2}{5}$; 23$\frac{4}{5}$; 24$\frac{2}{5}$; 25$\frac{1}{5}$; 12$\frac{2}{5}$. The horses in contention to the six-furlong marker were Krieger, J W Black, and Lots of Truth.

SEVENTH RACE

Saratoga

AUGUST 3, 2001

1⅛ MILES. (Inner Turf)(1.46¹) ALLOWANCE. Purse $44,000. (Up To $8,536 NYSBFOA) For Three Year Olds And Upward Which Have Never Won Two Races. Three Year Olds 118 lbs.; Older 122 lbs. Non–winners of a race at a mile or over on the turf since June 15 allowed, 2 lbs. (Races where entered for $50,000 or less not considered in allowances). (Preference by condition eligibility).

Value of Race: $44,000 Winner $26,400; second $8,800; third $4,840; fourth $2,640; fifth $1,320. Mutuel Pool $655,069.00 Exacta Pool $638,251.00 Trifecta Pool $460,525.00

Last Raced	Horse	M/Eqt. A.Wt	PP	St	¼	½	¾	Str	Fin	Jockey	Odds $1
21Jun01 7Bel²	Krieger	Lb	3 116	5	1	1½	1½	1½	1⁷	1¾	Chavez J F	1.70
4Jly01 6Bel¹	Blazing Fury	Lb	3 118	1	6	8½	10²½	8¹½	4hd	2³½	Migliore R	9.80
6Jly01 9Bel²	Gumshoe	Lb	4 120	8	5	5¹	5hd	6hd	5hd	3hd	Espinoza J L	a–10.90
21Jun01 4Bel¹	Dubai To Dubai	Lb	3 118	4	4	4hd	4¹½	4¹½	3hd	4nk	Castellano J J	5.40
14Jly01 4Del²	Dicken's Storm	L	4 120	7	2	6½	7²½	7²½	2hd	5⁴½	Prado E S	20.00
27Jun01 5Bel³	Active Cat	Lb	3 116	12	12	12	12	12	8½	6¹¼	Leon F	24.75
1Jly01 7Bel⁹	J W Black		3 116	2	3	2hd	2⁵	3¹½	6²½	7¹½	Davis R G	33.50
11Jly01 4Del⁸	Who Luvs You Baby	L	5 120	3	7	11²½	11⁴½	11½	12	8¹	Guidry M	a–10.90
1Jly01 7Bel⁴	Lots Of Truth	L	3 116	11	10	3½	3hd	5hd	9½	9nk	Velazquez J R	6.80
6Jly01 9Bel⁵	Hightouch	Lf	3 116	9	9	7hd	8²	9²	10hd10no		Gryder A T	19.20
22Jun01 9Bel⁸	Impressionist	L	3 116	6	8	9hd	9½	10²½	11½	11nk	Samyn J L	16.70
21Jun01 7Bel¹¹	Stone Age	L	3 116	10	11	10²	6½	2hd	7²½12		Bailey J D	7.60

a–Coupled: Gumshoe and Who Luvs You Baby.

OFF AT 4:14 Start Good. Won driving. Course firm.

TIME :22², :46¹, 1:10³, 1:35⁴, 1:48¹ (:22.43, :46.23, 1:10.69, 1:35.90, 1:48.29)

$2 Mutuel Prices:

5–KRIEGER	5.40	3.60	3.10
2–BLAZING FURY		9.10	6.70
1A–GUMSHOE (a–entry)			4.70

$2 EXACTA 5–2 PAID $45.80 $2 TRIFECTA 5–2–1 PAID $251.50

Ch. c, (Feb), by Lord At War*Arg–Abigailthewife, by Affirmed. Trainer Orseno Joseph. Bred by Adena Springs (Ky).

KRIEGER contested the pace from the outside, drew away when roused and was kept to a drive to the finish. BLAZING FURY was hustled along inside, came wide into the stretch and finished gamely but could not get to the winner. GUMSHOE chased the pace along the inside and had no rally. DUBAI TO DUBAI chased the pace from the outside and lacked a rally. DICKEN'S STORM raced close up early, put in a four wide run on the second turn and faded in the stretch. ACTIVE CAT broke through the gate prior to the start and was never a factor during the running. J W BLACK contested the pace along the inside and tired in the stretch. WHO LUVS YOU BABY raced inside and had no rally. LOTS OF TRUTH broke through the gate before the start and tired after showing brief speed. HIGHTOUCH had no response when roused. IMPRESSIONIST raced inside and tired. STONE AGE was outrun.

Owners— 1, Stronach Stable; 2, Kimmel Caesar P & Nicholson Ronald; 3, Nielsen Jeffrey L; 4, Godolphin Inc; 5, Denlea Park Stable Goodman Gerald &; 6, Evans Edward P; 7, Shanley Michael & Weiss Steve; 8, Pont Street Stable; 9, Lacombe Stables; 10, Gold Spur Stable; 11, Karches Peter F & Rankowitz Michael; 12, Stonerside Stable

Trainers—1, Orseno Joseph; 2, Toner James J; 3, Carroll Del W II; 4, Suroor Saeed bin; 5, Pregman John S Jr; 6, Hennig Mark; 7, Schulhofer Flint S; 8, Carroll Del W II; 9, Pletcher Todd A; 10, Lewis Lisa L; 11, Clement Christophe; 12, Mott William I

Scratched— Northwest Hill (28Jun01 7CD⁵), Diversification (21Jun01 7BEL¹⁰), Crazed (1Jly01 1BEL⁵), Al Barrak (9Jly01 2CRC³)

$2 Pick Three (1–1–5) Paid $82.00; Pick Three Pool $108,535.

Krieger went on to win the race at odds of about 2-1. But note that the horses in contention during the better part of this race, J W Black and Lots Of Truth, went off at odds of about 33-1 and 6-1, respectively. Furthermore, note that Krieger, Blazing Fury, Gumshoe, Dubai To Dubai, and Dicken's Storm all ran well and were coming out of races where they finished either first or second. Look at their prior-race finishes, which were highlighted on the race-result chart.

What makes this so eye-opening is that, with the exception of wire-to-wire winner Krieger, J W Black had them all beat for three quarters of a mile before weakening into the stretch. In addition, the best fractions of this race were recorded while J W Black was ahead of all these well-meant horses. Adding all these facts together, doesn't this make J W Black a very interesting horse for us to look for going into his next race?

Check out this next chart—it's a true thing of beauty.

FIFTH RACE

Saratoga

AUGUST 30, 2001

1 1/16 MILES. (Turf)(1.38 4) CLAIMING. Purse $46,000. (Up To $8,924 NYSBFOA) For Three Year Olds. Weight 122 lbs. Non–winners of two races at a mile or over since June 22 allowed, 2 lbs. A race at a mile or over on the turf since then, 4 lbs. CLAIMING PRICE $75,000, for each $5,000 to $65,000 1 lbs. (Races where entered for $50,000 or less not considered). (Winners preferred).

Value of Race: $46,000 Winner $27,600; second $9,200; third $5,060; fourth $2,760; fifth $1,380. Mutuel Pool $456,158.00 Exacta Pool $476,760.00 Trifecta Pool $372,718.00

Last Raced	Horse	M/Eqt.	A	Wt	PP	St	1/4	1/2	3/4	Str	Fin	Jockey	Cl'g Pr	Odds $1
3Aug01 7Sar7	J W Black		3	118	2	3	3hd	41	4 1/2	4hd	1hd	Castellano J J	75000	22.80
4Aug01 5Sar2	Gail's Drive	L	3	118	7	7	72	61	61	5 1/2	2 1/2	Davis R G	75000	7.60
4Aug01 8Sar4	Delta Wheel	L	3	118	8	10	9 2 1/2	9 3 1/2	7 2 1/2	6hd	3hd	Bailey J D	75000	3.70
30Jly01 1Sar1	Homecooking Ruby	Lb	3	116	4	1	1 1/2	22	1hd	1 1/2	4 2 1/2	Chavez J F	65000	3.60
3Aug01 7Sar6	Active Cat	Lb	3	118	1	4	10	10	10	9 1/2	5hd	Migliore R	75000	9.90
4Aug01 5Sar3	Tom's Thunder	b	3	118	3	2	4 1/2	3hd	3 1/2	2hd	6 1/2	Prado E S	75000	11.90
4Aug01 8Sar9	Tremmor	L	3	118	9	9	8hd	8 1/2	8 1/2	7 1 1/2	7 3/4	Day P	75000	4.70
3Aug01 7Sar9	Lots Of Truth	L	3	118	10	8	2 1 1/2	1hd	2hd	3 1/2	8 1/2	Velazquez J R	75000	11.50
6Jly01 9Rel8	Gem Of A Guy	Lb	3	118	6	5	62	7 1/2	91	10	9 1/2	Guidry M	75000	32.75
11Aug01 5Sar6	Faiths Wish		3	118	5	6	5 1 1/2	5 2 1/2	5 1/2	8hd10		Gryder A T	75000	6.90

OFF AT 3:09 Start Good. Won driving. Course firm.

TIME :23 2, :46 3, 1:10, 1:34 4, 1:41 (:23.47, :46.74, 1:10.05, 1:34.92, 1:41.01)

$2 Mutuel Prices:

3–J W BLACK	47.60	23.20	12.80
7–GAIL'S DRIVE		10.00	5.70
8–DELTA WHEEL			3.90

$2 EXACTA 3–7 PAID $417.50 $2 TRIFECTA 3–7–8 PAID $3,493.00

B. c, (Mar), by Cozzene–Liberia, by Miswaki. Trainer Schulhofer Flint S. Bred by Palides Investments N V Inc (Ky).

J W BLACK raced close up inside, came wide into the stretch, dug in gamely and prevailed under a drive. GAIL'S DRIVE was outrun early, rallied four wide on the second turn and finished gamely outside. DELTA WHEEL was outrun early, rallied four wide and good finish outside. HOMECOOKING RUBY quickly showed in front, set the pace and weakened in the final furlong. ACTIVE CAT was outrun early, came wide for the drive and offered a mild rally outside. TOM'S THUNDER raced close up outside, put in a three wide run approaching the stretch and faltered in the final furlong. TREMMOR raced inside and had no rally. LOTS OF TRUTH contested the pace from the outside and tired in the stretch. GEM OF A GUY had no rally. FAITHS WISH chased the pace and tired after three quarters.

Owners— 1, Shanley Michael & Weiss Steve; 2, Willmott Stables; 3, Farish William S & Hudson Edward J; 4, Our Sugar Bear Stable; 5, Evans Edward P; 6, Schwartz Herbert T & Carol A; 7, Snowden Diane & Guy B; 8, Lacombe Stables; 9, Stronach Stable; 10, Carey Thomas M

Trainers—1, Schulhofer Flint S; 2, Reinstedler Anthony; 3, Howard Neil J; 4, Martin Carlos F; 5, Hennig Mark; 6, Schwartz Scott M; 7, Mott William I; 8, Pletcher Todd A; 9, Orseno Joseph; 10, Vestal Peter M

Delta Wheel was claimed by Dubb Michael; trainer, Donk David.,

Tremmor was claimed by Team Canonie Inc; trainer, Hough Stanley M.,

Faiths Wish was claimed by Ramsey Kenneth L; trainer, Simon Charles.

Scratched— Kentucky Squall (17Aug01 5SAR3), Stauch (4Aug01 5SAR5), Northwest Hill (26Aug01 10SAR2), Amarettitorumble (17Aug01 5SAR2)

$2 Daily Double (5–3) Paid $123.00; Daily Double Pool $116,173.

$2 Pick Three (6–5–3) Paid $513.00; Pick Three Pool $97,293.

In this case, the performance angles were pretty evident to anyone who took notice of such information offered through the race-result charts. If you were being thorough as you read your charts, you would have realized that J W Black had nearly all these horses beat for three quarters of a mile under quick fractional times before weakening. Being thorough becomes kind of a built-in safety net for all those who are patient, persistent, and do their homework.

10

CHART CHECKLIST

THE FOLLOWING IS a checklist of items and factors that should be reviewed and noted while adding information to a race chart, as well as topics that should be considered before making an investment.

Each listed factor should be considered, highlighted, explained, and commented on in order to achieve top results while keeping race-result charts. Remember, the more information that is added to a race-result chart, the more valuable each chart becomes.

1) 23⅗ opening quarter for routes, or quicker

2) 22⅗ opening quarter for sprints, or quicker

3) 24–second quarters within, or quicker

4) 12–second eighths within, or quicker

5) 6–second sixteenths within, or quicker

6) Projected key race

7) Tough post positions

8) Trip notes as well as troubled trips

9) Good finishes

10) Middle moves

11) Good early speed

12) Prior finish positions

13) Each horse's last finish position

14) Race comparisons on same race card

15) Today's weather conditions—last rained?

16) How track was playing in general—bias?

17) Wind conditions

18) Track variant

I realize that there is a lot of possible information that can be added to each race chart, and I also realize that this can create a tricky situation. Sometimes there is just too much information being offered, and one may have trouble pinning down the angle or factor that might reflect the greatest edge within a race.

With practice and experience, one will be able to judge which angles and factors are the most relevant in any key racing situation. Unfortunately, we just can't list which angles and factors should be used instead of others before we read and interpret exactly what the past performances and race charts are trying to tell us. This judgment has to come from each of us as we interpret each racing situation.

If there were one constant set of angles that should always be selected over any other, however, I believe that they would be performance angles, because performance equals ability and ability wins races.

I realize that it will take a lot of time and effort to try and add this wealth of information to each day's race-result charts, but I assure you that in the long run, you will find that all the work and dedication pay off.

11

WORKING
THE CHARTS

NOW THAT YOU'RE armed with all this race information you have been creating and compiling, it's time to put this method into action.

The best way to start is by handicapping each race in your usual manner. Use your traditional methods and angles to create a list of contenders. Always give added consideration to any horses that are getting an equipment change or making a surface switch. These simple changes can turn a horse around very quickly and usually can improve a horse's performance within a single race. This might be that race.

After handicapping a race and creating a list of horses that you feel have a chance to run well today, the next step would be to go to your result charts and research each contender's last start. Check each race chart for any key information you might have added to an individual horse's prior efforts. Sometimes you may have to go farther back through your charts and look at several previous races to get a clearer picture of just how a horse might be coming into today's event.

The next step is to go through the rest of today's field and research each horse's last race through your race-result charts. These horses may not have come up as contenders when you first handicapped today's race, but we should still research their last starts. It always pays to be thorough in these situations. Any critical information you might have added to an earlier race chart could make a huge difference in today's contest.

For example, you just might include a horse in an exacta today because you realized that your note about him having "nowhere to go the entire stretch" last time out moved him up in your estimation against today's field. Instead of thinking that this horse turned in a flat race last time out, you might now give him the benefit of the doubt and deem him to be in a sharper state of current condition than first thought.

Now, while having all this critical data is great, it also sets a trap for a handicapper. All this stored information might create some confusion about how to use it. One can get muddled and not be able to decipher which angles and information are the most critical.

The easiest way to avoid confusion is to be methodical. Handicap in steps and stay focused on the race at hand. Here is a list of how to methodically go about adding the methodology of charting races to your daily handicapping practices.

- Create a list of contenders using your best handicapping methods.
- Include horses that have equipment and surface changes to this list.
- Go through the race-result charts to research each contender's last start.
- Decide if the information from the result charts adds any strength to any of the listed contenders.
- Consider if any contender has a decided or likable edge within today's field.
- Research the rest of the field's prior race charts to see if any information might move a horse up within today's field.
- Weigh out all the angles and options, which should bring you to your final decisions within today's racing situation.

Being methodical can help for a few different reasons. It can help keep your thinking straight and help you become more accurate. And if you do get confused for any reason or stumble onto something and lose your train of thought, by being methodical, you can always go back and retrace your steps.

Earlier, for the purposes of clarification, I stated that the best way to start handicapping a race involving this method is to first use your own personal methods. You need some type of process of elimination to narrow down a given field to a short list of contenders. Your handicapping either has to take away lesser horses, leaving the better ones in the field, or has to select the better horses so you can discard the weaker. When you then apply the next step of researching each contender's last start and you find more positive information on any of these contenders, you are actually raising this group of horses to another level.

Understand that you can successfully use this method of gathering information off the race charts solely as your main approach to handicapping. But you will have situations where more than one horse in a race has positive information taken off the race charts. When this happens you will have to either separate these contenders in some way or use all of them in your wagers.

What I like to do for my own personal handicapping is first to narrow down every field to a few contenders that have a pace edge against the rest of today's field. Whether that advantage takes the form of early speed, final time, or an overall pace average, once a horse has an edge in one of these areas, he gets lifted up a notch against today's field. Then if I can gather positive information off the result charts, this horse gets moved up another notch in my mind.

Here a notch obviously represents an edge, and once a horse has a double edge going for him, my level of confidence rises pretty high. If I could find just one such horse once a week, I would be a pretty happy handicapper.

12

READY TO FIRE

ANOTHER PART OF working the charts is being able to spot a horse that figures to run a big race today based on the performance of another horse that came out of the same race and returned with a superior effort. In fact, while researching the race chart of today's horse in question, you may find that several other horses exiting the same event have already returned and run big races.

If this is the case, then we have something to work with. Note the running styles of the horses that ran well next time out. Were they near the lead or off the pace in their previous race? Did the horse you are researching for today's event run a race similar to those who returned with big efforts?

You don't always need what we have defined as a key race, one in which several horses coming out of the same contest all return with big races next time out. Sometimes all you need is just one horse to come back and run well. Of course, we still must figure how, and if, this horse fits today's race, based on several different aspects.

The first step is to look at the horse that already returned with the big effort and figure out what he showed in the prior race. There should already be some trip notes, surface notes, highlighted fractional times, and other added information on the race chart.

While going back to look over the previous race chart, note if there were any horses already highlighted for any reasons, such as racing close up to a better-than-normal pace. Perhaps a horse was highlighted for making a good middle move or for turning in a big finish. Perhaps several horses raced from poor post positions.

Ideally you want to discover that the horse that returned was already highlighted and that today's horse ran a very similar race. If this is not the case, and you are dealing with two completely different types of running lines, then the next step is to examine this race for quality. Go through the other races run on the same card and investigate if this race was one of the better ones run that day.

Take a look at the following race scenario: I am handicapping the sixth race at Belmont Park on June 12, 2002. I feel that a horse named Sonata Cosmos figures to run a big race today; she has enough ability to top this field and is in a sneaky-sharp state of current condition, since she just had one race off a layoff dated May 15, which was about four weeks ago.

My next step is to research her last start among my race-result charts. The goal now is to see if I can find any further information within the prior race-result charts to make her case in today's event a little stronger. On the other hand, finding more information might help prevent me from making a bad investment. In this game, being thorough can help in several ways.

Going back to her prior race on May 15, 2002—Race 7 at Belmont—I find that I had made several notes that day regarding a couple of horses' running lines, in addition to having made surface notes. Furthermore, I had indicated that one horse had come out of the May 15 race and won in her next start.

Rained overnight into today   *22 variant*

RACE 7 Bel–15May02 1 1/16 Miles⊤(1.38²), 3 ↑ Ⓕ Alw 46000n1x

Value of Race: $46,000. 1st $27,600; 2nd $9,200; 3rd $5,060; 4th $2,760; 5th $1,380. Mutuel
Pools: $359,335, Ex $311,997, Tri $248,774, DD $78,691, Pick–3 $69,604

Last Raced	Horse	M/Eq	A	Wt	PP	St	1/4	1/2	3/4	Str	Fin	Odds$1	
19Apr02 5Kee³	Tarnished Lady	L	3	115	2	8	9½	9½	7¹	3½	1hd	3.05	*–8 wide and Flying*
21Aug01 Dea¹²	Polyandry-IR	L	4	122	5	10	10	8hd	6hd	2hd	2³½	2.00	
17Mar02 ¹¹Tam⁵	Miss Halory	L	3	115	9	5	3hd	4½	4¹½	1hd	3¹	4.20	*Good finish*
21Nov01 6Lrl³	La Fontainiere-IR	L	4	122	6	7	6½	5hd	5hd	7³½	4¹½	15.80	*–1*
17Nov01 3Aqu¹	Ms. Rapunzel	L	4	122	3	3	4½	3hd	3hd	4½	5¹½	8.90	
17Apr02 6GP²	Call An Audible	L	3	115	8	4	2½	2hd	2hd	6¹	6½	8.10	*Blocked on turn Full*
19Dec01 8Aqu⁷	Sonata Cosmos	Lf	4	122	4	1	1½	1²½	1hd	5hd	7hd	36.75	*of run*
28Apr02 7Aqu³	Terri's Toy	L	4	122	10	6	7½	7½	8½	8³½	8³	61.25	
28Apr02 7Aqu⁴	Barrister Kathleen	Lb	3	115	7	9	8hd	10	10	9hd	9²½	23.60	
28Apr02 7Aqu²	Serene Ditty	Lf	4	122	1	2	5hd	6hd	9¹½	10	10	21.00	

OFF 4:10 Start Good. Won driving. Course good.   *243 243 242 234 6*

TIME :243, :491, 1:133, 1:372, 1:432 (:24.74, :49.22, 1:13.68, 1:37.53, 1:43.52)

2 – TARNISHED LADY	8.10	4.10	2.90
5 – POLYANDRY-IR		3.50	2.80
9 – MISS HALORY			3.40

$2 Ex (2-5) 37.20 $2 Tri (2-5-9) 101.50 $2 DD (6-2) 52.00
$2 Pick-3 (1-6-2) 773.00

Ch. f, (Apr), by Lord Avie–Tarnished Gold, by Cabrini Green. Trainer Pletcher Todd A. Bred by North Wales LLC (Ky).

TARNISHED LADY was rated along inside, swung wide entering the stretch, dug in gamely outside and prevailed under a drive. POLYANDRY (IRE) was rated along early, came wide nearing the stretch and finished gamely. MISS HALORY raced with the pace while four wide, rallied to gain a short lead in midstretch and weakened late. LA FONTAINIERE (IRE) was rated inside, altered course when caught in traffic in the stretch and had no rally. MS. RAPUNZEL raced close up inside, put in a run along the inside on the turn and tired in the final furlong. CALL AN AUDIBLE raced with the pace from the outside and tired in the stretch. SONATA COSMOS quickly showed in front, set the pace and tired in the stretch. TERRI'S TOY tired after a four wide trip. BARRISTER KATHLEEN raced wide throughout and tired. SERENE DITTY raced inside and tired.

Jockeys— 1, Velazquez J R; 2, Santos J A; 3, Bailey J D; 4, Arroyo N Jr; 5, Gryder A T; 6, Migliore R; 7, Davis R G; 8, Castillo H Jr; 9, Carr D; 10, Prado E S

Trainers— 1, Pletcher Todd A; 2, Clement Christophe; 3, Mott William I; 4, Pugh Peter D; 5, Levine Bruce N; 6, Hennig Mark; 7, Morrison John; 8, Ritvo Timothy; 9, Barbara Robert; 10, Serpe Philip M

Owners— 1, Anstu Stables; 2, de Rothschild Edouard; 3, Stonerside Stable; 4, Happy Hill Farm; 5, Four Drake Stable; 6, Amerman Racing Stables; 7, Tucker Jeffrey; 8, Gordon Samuel; 9, Sabine Stable & Kelly Robert; 10, Dee John T Ryan Thomas F Moran Tom

Scratched— Prime Queen (13Apr02 6AQU²), Climbeverymountain (24Aug01 1SAR⁵), Sandra's Song (13Apr02 6AQU⁸), Sugar Dipped (4Apr02 6GP¹), A. P. Interest (21Apr02 2AQU¹) Go In (28Apr02 7AQU³)

Let's start with the surface notes. They say that it rained overnight into the next day (May 15), and the turf course was labeled good. So it figured that the fractional and final times on this turf course would be slow, since the course was soft, and that it was tougher than normal for a speed type to last on the lead.

Note that the fractional splits were slow in the early going, but the final fractions were solid. Highlighted for their performances were Sonata Cosmos, Ms. Rapunzel, Call An Audible, and Miss Halory. Although they were not highlighted for running close to the better fractional splits (which were the final two fractions), they were highlighted for dueling on the front end. Since the turf course was on the soft side, I gave more leeway for the early fractional times being a little slow. Here I felt that the slower recorded fractions were deceiving. More credit should have been given to the horses near the early lead due to the slower surface conditions.

What gives strength to this theory is the fact that Ms. Rapunzel had already come out of this race and won, as I had noted on this chart. Ms. Rapunzel had been highlighted after this May 15 race because she was in the thick of it early.

RACE 8 Bel–5Jun02 1 Mile⊤(1.31³), 3↑ⒻAlw 46000n1x

Value of Race: $46,000. 1st $27,600; 2nd $9,200; 3rd $5,060; 4th $2,760; 5th $1,380. Mutuel Pools: $358,232, Ex $311,224, Tri $247,905, Pick–6 $60,137 Carryover $36,082

Last Raced	Horse	M/Eq	A	Wt	PP	St	¼	½	¾	Str	Fin	Odds$1
15May02 7Bel⁵	Ms. Rapunzel	L	4	121	5	6	5½	6¹	5hd	2hd	1¾	11.10
13Apr02 6Aqu²	Prime Queen	Lb	4	121	4	2	11½	12½	11½	1²	2no	7.90
17May02 7Bel⁴	Hottentot	Lf	3	115	9	4	4½	3hd	2½	3½	3½	3.65
9May02 4Bel¹	Pieria	L	3	117	1	10	7hd	7½	8⁶	6⁸	4½	1.30
6Dec01 7Aqu¹⁰	Time For Faith	L	4	121	2	9	8½	8½	7½	5hd	5nk	15.50
13Apr02 6Aqu⁸	Sandra's Song	Lb	4	121	7	8	10	10	4hd	4½	6⁹	10.10
1May02 2Aqu⁴	Database	L	3	115	10	7	9²	9hd	9¹⁰	9	7¾	18.80
11May02 8Bel⁶	Lyrical Prado	Lf	3	115	6	3	2½	2½	3½	7²	8²	26.50
16May02 9Bel⁴	Chasing Lightning	L	3	117	8	5	6hd	5½	6hd	8¹	9	15.00
6Dec01 7Aqu⁹	Five To Four	L	4	121	3	1	3hd	4hd	10	—	—	38.25

Five To Four:Eased;

OFF 4:40 Start Good. Won driving. Course firm.
TIME :23¹, :46², 1:11¹, 1:34¹ (:23.29, :46.55, 1:11.26, 1:34.34)

5–MS. RAPUNZEL	24.20	12.20	6.90
4–PRIME QUEEN		8.10	4.70
10–HOTTENTOT			3.70

$2 Ex (5–4) 148.00 $2 Tri (5-4-10) 616.00
$2 Pick-6 (7-7-2-9-1-5) 5 Correct 601.00

Ch. f, by Whitney Tower–Hail a Princess, by Hail the Ruckus. Trainer Levine Bruce N. Bred by Norman Dellheim & Gary J Mesnick (Fla).

MS. RAPUNZEL raced in hand while between rivals early, responded when roused in upper stretch, dug in gamely and prevailed, driving. PRIME QUEEN quickly opened a clear lead, set the pace and dug in gamely along the inside in the stretch. HOTTENTOT raced close up while three wide and finished gamely. PIERIA was outrun early, came wide for the drive and was going well late. TIME FOR FAITH was rated along inside, rallied turning for home and finished well inside. SANDRA'S SONG was outrun early, put in a five wide run nearing the stretch and lacked a solid finishing kick. DATABASE raced wide and had no rally. LYRICAL PRADO chased the pace from the outside and tired. CHASING LIGHTNING raced four wide and tired in the stretch. FIVE TO FOUR showed speed along the inside, stopped and was eased in the stretch.

Jockeys— 1, Gryder A T; 2, Migliore R; 3, Velazquez J R; 4, Bailey J D; 5, Santos J A; 6, Espinoza J L; 7, Prado E S; 8, Castillo H Jr; 9, Chavez J F; 10, Luzzi M J

Trainers– 1, Levine Bruce N; 2, Iwinski Allen; 3, Pletcher Todd A; 4, Mott William I; 5, O'Brien Leo; 6, Tagg Barclay; 7, McGaughey Claude III; 8, Campo John P Jr; 9, Gullo Gary P; 10, Violette Richard A Jr

Owners— 1, Four Drake Stable; 2, Amendola Robert J; 3, Dogwood Stable; 4, Hickory Tree Stable; 5, Literary Lion Farm; 6, Melillo George & Sandra; 7, Janney III Stuart S; 8, Collier Reginald B; 9, Manorwood Stables & Valenti Anthony; 10, Violette Richard A Jr

Scratched— Dynamite Miss (12May02 5BEL³), Sunset Express (12May02 5BEL²), Soixante Dix (16May02 6BEL¹), La Fontainiere (15May02 7BEL⁴), Saintly Action (25May02 6BEL⁸), Paugus Bay (11May02 3BEL⁶)

Since Ms. Rapunzel had been highlighted for being near the early lead on May 15 and came out of that event to win, it would be great to find another horse in today's race that was also a factor in the early going in that race. Sonata Cosmos fits the bill, since she dueled on the early lead ahead of Ms. Rapunzel for three quarters of a mile.

RACE 6 Bel–12Jun02 1⅛ Miles (I–Turf)(1.45³), 3 ↑ Ⓕ Alw 46000n1x

Value of Race: $46,000. 1st $27,600; 2nd $9,200; 3rd $5,060; 4th $2,760; 5th $1,380. Mutuel Pools: $352,500, Ex $349,412, Tri $279,857, Pick–3 $51,947

Last Raced	Horse	M/Eq	A	Wt	PP	St	¼	½	¾	Str	Fin	Odds$1
15May02 7Bel⁷	Sonata Cosmos	Lf	4	121	5	1	1¹	1¹	1½	13½	1³	23.80
23May02 5Bel¹	Miss Playbill	L	3	117	1	2	32½	31½	3½	2½	2½	1.25
19Oct01 9Bel⁶	Sky Cover	L	4	121	6	8	4½	4¹	4½	31½	31¼	6.50
17May02 7Bel⁶	Dynamic Lady	Lb	3	115	7	3	6hd	71½	7hd	4½	4hd	8.30
20Sep01 1Bel⁷	Zoomer	Lb	4	121	3	5	51½	5½	51½	5hd	5½	48.50
17May02 7Bel³	Attico	L	3	115	2	7	9	9	85½	71½	61¼	4.70
27May02 4Bel⁴	Bluebird Day-IR	L	3	115	9	4	2½	2½	2½	6¹	7¾	5.80
21Jly01 New⁹	Tjinouska	L	4	121	8	9	7²	6½	6½	8¹⁵	816¾	12.20
20Sep01 1Bel¹⁰	Rememberance	L	4	121	4	6	8½	8½	9	9	9	40.50

OFF 3:37 Start Good. Won driving. Course firm.
TIME :24³, :49¹, 1:14, 1:38¹, 1:49³ (:24.72, :49.39, 1:14.18, 1:38.32, 1:49.67)

5–SONATA COSMOS	49.60	14.40	10.20
1–MISS PLAYBILL		3.20	2.60
6–SKY COVER			5.30

$2 Ex (5-1) 202.00 $2 Tri (5-1-6) 1,380.00 $2 Pick-3 (6-4-5) 1,657.00

Gr/ro f, by Bien Bien–Ashley's Love, by Alydar. Trainer Morrison John. Bred by John A Toffan & Trudy McCaffery (Ky).

SONATA COSMOS soon opened a clear lead, made the pace, opened up in the stretch and was driving under the line. MISS PLAYBILL showed speed along the inside while in hand and rallied to get the place spot. SKY COVER was unhurried early on, rallied three wide on the second turn and finished well outside. DYNAMIC LADY was rated along inside and lacked a rally. ZOOMER had no response when roused. ATTICO was outrun early, put in a four wide run on the second turn and lacked a solid finishing kick. BLUEBIRD DAY (IRE) attended the pace from the outside and tired. TJINOUSKA had no rally. REMEMBERANCE raced wide and tired.

Jockeys— 1, Castellano J J; 2, Bailey J D; 3, Chavez J F; 4, Gryder A T; 5, Espinoza J L; 6, Bridgmohan S X; 7, Prado E S; 8, Santos J A; 9, Castillo H Jr

Trainers– 1, Morrison John; 2, Mott William I; 3, Dupps Kristina; 4, Badgett William Jr; 5, Kelly Patrick J; 6, Bush Thomas M; 7, Arnold George R II; 8, Clement Christophe; 9, Skiffington Thomas J

Owners— 1, Tucker Jeffrey; 2, Centennial Farms; 3, Picwynn Stables; 4, C K Woods Stable; 5, Fox Ridge Farm Inc; 6, Wertheimer Farm; 7, Humphrey G W Jr; 8, Jan Steinmann; 9, Phillips Joan G & John W

Scratched— Jilbab (16May02 4BEL²), New Dice (25May02 5MTH¹)

This is another approach to handicapping using race-result charts, one that is based on the performances and results of other horses. Here we created an angle to find other sharply conditioned horses whose truest form might be hidden.

13

FINISHED PRODUCT

THE FOLLOWING CHART contains a sample of the possible information one can add to a race-result chart. Remember, the depth and quality of all the added information solely depends on the keeper of the charts.

Surface Seems Honest today Prior to this race

No Bias Last 3 days

No Rain in 5 Days

-15 variant

Tough Posts

FOURTH RACE
Saratoga
AUGUST 3, 2001

1 1/16 MILES. (Turf)(1.384) MAIDEN SPECIAL WEIGHT. Purse $42,000. For Maiden Three Year Olds And Upward, foaled in New York State and approved by the New York State–Bred Registry. Three Year Olds 118 lbs.; Older 122 lbs. (Non–starters for a claiming price less than $35,000 in the last three starts preferred).

Value of Race: $42,000 Winner $25,200; second $8,400; third $4,620; fourth $2,520; fifth $1,260. Mutuel Pool $455,906.00 Exacta Pool $492,880.00 Quinella Pool $50,388.00 Trifecta Pool $363,499.00

Last Raced	Horse	M/Eqt.	A.	Wt	PP	St	¼	½	¾	Str	Fin	Jockey	Odds $1
7Jly01 5Del8	Malagash — *3*	L	3	118	7	4	4½	4½	2hd	2hd	1nk	Samyn J L	2.60
29Jun01 4Bel6	Quiet Ruler — *1*	L	3	118	12	10	6hd	7hd	5½	41½	21¾	Prado E S	12.50
13Jly01 9Bel3	Mohawk Marty	L	3	118	10	9	2hd	2hd	32	32	3½	Day P	8.50
8Jly01 1FL2	Tommy Lees Shadow	Lbf	4	122	8	5	1½	1½	1½	12	41¼	Espinoza J L	47.75
13Jly01 3Rkm6	New York Jazz	Lb	4	122	9	7	9hd	82½	7hd	62½	51½	Gryder A T	14.80
7Jly01 9Bel11	Slewganis — *2*	L	3	118	2	1	32	31½	4½	5½	6½	Toscano P R	77.50
24Nov00 3Aqu12	Heated Exchange	L	3	118	4	3	7½	52	61	72	71	Velazquez J R	7.30
13Apr01 3Aqu10	Impavid	Lb	3	118	1	8	101½	113½	9½	8hd	82¼	Meche D J	29.50
21Jly01 5Bel3	Vandiano	Lf	3	118	6	6	112½	10hd	105	103½	9hd	Castellano J J	7.80
29Apr01 1Aqu3	Jeopardy Blue	L	4	122	11	11	51	6½	81½	92	105¼	Chavez J F	3.10
	Angie's Reason	b	3	118	3	12	12	12	115½	116	114¾	Pitty C D	59.00
4Jly01 1Bel8	Rare Prince	Lb	4	122	5	2	81½	9hd	12	12	12	Migliore R	10.80

OFF AT 2:36 Start Good. Won driving. Course firm.

23¹ 24³ 24² 24² 6¹

TIME :231, :474, 1:121, 1:363, 1:424 (:23.24, :47.80, 1:12.36, 1:36.76, 1:42.95)

$2 Mutuel Prices:

7–MALAGASH	7.20	4.90	3.50
12–QUIET RULER		9.80	7.10
10–MOHAWK MARTY			4.80

$2 EXACTA 7–12 PAID $104.00 $2 QUINELLA 7–12 PAID $73.00 $2 TRIFECTA 7–12–10 PAID $659.00

B. g, (Apr), by Signal Tap–Senorita Constanza, by His Majesty. Trainer Voss Thomas H. Bred by Michelotti John R (NY).

MALAGASH raced close up early, responded when roused, dug in determinedly in the stretch and prevailed under a drive. QUIET RULER rallied turning for home and finished gamely outside. MOHAWK MARTY raced with the pace from the outside, rallied inside into the stretch, was steadied along the inside in deep stretch, altered course and finished gamely. TOMMY LEES SHADOW quickly showed in front, set the pace, drew clear in the stretch and weakened in the final furlong. NEW YORK JAZZ was rated along early, came wide for the drive and offered a mild rally outside. SLEWGANIS had no rally. HEATED EXCHANGE raced inside and had no rally. IMPAVID raced wide and had no rally. VANDIANO had no response when roused. JEOPARDY BLUE chased outside and tired. ANGIE'S REASON was outrun. RARE PRINCE tired.

Owners— 1, Voss Mrs Thomas H; 2, Cornerstone Stable & Old Brookside; 3, Summer Wind Stable; 4, Bedinotti Peter; 5, Ostrager Barry R; 6, LeBlanc Kirsten; 7, Flying Zee Stable; 8, Wolf Carl A; 9, Broman Chester & Mary R Sr; 10, Kevmar Stable; 11, Pond View Stable; 12, Mann Maria

Trainers— 1, Voss Thomas H; 2, Mueller Russell; 3, Hertler John O; 4, Henry Neville; 5, Levine Bruce N; 6, Everett Scott; 7, Serpe Philip M; 8, Matties Gregg M; 9, Hernandez Ramon M; 10, Sciacca Gary; 11, Schettino Dominick A; 12, Barbara Robert

Scratched— Thesonofthesun (21Jly01 5BEL7), Lord Buckley (13Jly01 9BEL6), El Machete (20Jly01 6BEL7), Sir Prado (4Jly01 2LS5)

$2 Pick Three (4–3–7) Paid $123.00; Pick Three Pool $131,677.

Steadied Stretch, Altered course, Would have been closer at finish

Solid opening, Slow Middle Good finish

Fastest turf race of day on Final time -VS- ANIX + ANZX horses

14

THE VALUE OF STUDYING COMPLETE RACE-RESULT CHARTS

DRF *Simulcast Weekly,* published by *Daily Racing Form,* includes complete result charts of virtually every major simulcast signal in the country—up to eleven in all. Below is a detailed explanation of several handicapping features included in these expanded charts, and how these features are helpful to the player who chooses to play either one track or multiple circuits.

1. **Detailed Trip Notes:** *DRF Simulcast Weekly* Official Charts contain a more detailed explanation of a horse's trip than the abbreviated line found in the past performances of *Daily Racing Form* or a track program. For example, the abridged comment in DRF for Sunshine Dreamer might read, "five wide turn." The full comment, however, in the

DRF Simulcast Weekly Official Charts informs the handicapper that "Sunshine Dreamer rated close off the rail, angled five wide making her bid from the quarter pole, closed well under a steady drive but was outfinished for place the final yards." The comment for Jill Rabbit in DRF might read, "led briefly, yielded." The full comment paints a much different scenario. "Jill Rabbit led briefly early then pressured the pace from the inside, dueled briefly clear entering the stretch, stayed game to the sixteenth pole then reluctantly yielded."

FIFTH RACE

Aqueduct

DECEMBER 13, 2002

6 FURLONGS. (Inner Dirt)(1.08²) CLAIMING. Purse $16,000. For Fillies Three Years Old. Weight 122 lbs. Non-winners of two races since October 18 allowed, 1 lbs. A race since then, 3 lbs. CLAIMING PRICE $16,000, for each $1,000 to $14,000 2 lbs. (Races where entered for $12,500 or less not considered). (Registered New York Breds allowed 3 lbs.).

Value of Race: $16,000. Winner $9,600; second $3,200; third $1,760; fourth $960; fifth $480. Mutuel Pool $317,819.00 Exacta Pool $315,603.00 Trifecta Pool $208,746.00

Last Raced	Horse	M/Eqt. A.Wt	PP	St	¼	½	Str	Fin	Jockey	Cl'g Pr	Odds $1
8Aug02 9Sar9	Queen Of Saratoga	Lb 3 114	6	2	2hd	31	1hd	1½	Lopez C C	14000	9.90
22Nov02 1Aqu4	O desadorable	L 3 119	8	8	91	6hd	5hd	2½	Luzzi M J	16000	13.10
22Nov02 1Aqu6	Sunshine Dreamer	L 3 121	7	10	6hd	4hd	41½	33	Nelson D	16000	10.30
23Oct02 1Aqu8	Jill Rabbit	Lf 3 115	3	3	31	1hd	21	4hd	Juarez A J Jr	14000	3.65
18Nov02 4Med2	Nice Little Girl	f 3 110	5	4	1hd	2hd	3hd	5nk	Ramos H G5	14000	15.90
9Nov02 4Del5	Pure Wild	Lb 3 119	9	6	5hd	7hd	73	61	Bridgmohan S X	16000	15.70
14Nov02 4Aqu7	Sea Of Hope	Lb 3 116	1	7	4½	5½	61½	74¼	Toscano P R	16000	57.00
22Nov02 1Aqu3	Sunset Express	Lb 3 119	11	1	7hd	83	8½	81	Gryder A T	16000	2.65
24Nov02 2Aqu6	Thislilgirlcanrun	Lb 3 119	4	9	11	11	102	9½	Migliore R	16000	a-2.55
15Mar02 1Aqu1	Sweep North	Lb 3 114	2	11	102	102	9hd10³½	Chavez Luis5	16000	a-2.55
13Sep02 5Bel8	Butterfly Dancer	Lb 3 119	10	5	81	9½	11	11	Rojas R I	16000	97.00

a-Coupled: Thislilgirlcanrun and Sweep North.

OFF AT 2:21 Start Good. Won driving. Track fast.

TIME :23¹, :46⁴, :59, 1:11⁴ (:23.28, :46.88, :59.14, 1:11.93)

$2 Mutuel Prices:	5–QUEEN OF SARATOGA	21.80	13.00	7.50
	7–O'DESADORABLE		15.40	9.20
	6–SUNSHINE DREAMER			6.40

$2 EXACTA 5–7 PAID $310.00 $2 TRIFECTA 5–7–6 PAID $2,073.00

B. f., (Mar), by Signal Tap-Superetta, by Saratoga Six. Trainer Parisella John. Bred by Questroyal Stud LLC & Gavin Murphy (NY).

QUEEN OF SARATOGA pressured the pace three wide, dueled from the top of the stretch, edged clear nearing the sixteenth pole then kept an edge under solid handling. O DESADORABLE rated back off the rail, was eased out making her bid entering the stretch, got up for place late and was gaining. SUNSHINE DREAMER raced close off the rail, angled five wide making her bid from the quarter pole, closed well under a steady drive but was outfinished for place the final yards. JILL RABBIT led briefly early then pressured the pace from the inside, dueled briefly clear entering the stretch, stayed game to the sixteenth pole then reluctantly yielded. NICE LITTLE GIRL set a pressured pace from between rivals, dropped back entering the stretch and leveled out the final furlong. PURE WILD rated close toward the outside, was steadied trying to get out on the turn and finished evenly. SEA OF HOPE chased the pace from the outside, was off the rail through the turn and offered no rally. THISLILGIRLCANRUN dropped back early. SWEEP NORTH showed no speed and offered no rally. BUTTERFLY DANCER chased the pace from the outside, steadied slightly nearing the turn then gave way.

Owners– 1, Kupferberg Saul J & Max; 2, Desadora Joan & Perdaris Dimitri J; 3, C D & G Stable; 4, Team Valor Stables; 5, Stonehearted Chic Stables; 6, Rottkamp John R; 7, Stellar Stable; 8, Misa Robert W Jr; 9, For The Kids Stable Foss Monty & Mo; 10, Equispeed Stable; 11, Our Dream Stable.

Trainers– 1, Parisella John; 2, Hough Stanley M; 3 Klesaris Robert P; 4, Galluscio Dominic G; 5, Jerkens Steven T; 6, Klesaris Steve; 7, Nolan Donna; 8, Friedman Mitchell; 9, Contessa Gary C; 10 Contessa Gary C; 11, Cuadra Victor

Jill Rabbit was claimed by C D & G Stable; trainer, Kesaris Robert P.,
Sea Of Hope was claimed by Moirano John; trainer, Contessa Gary C.,
Sweep North was claimed by Brice Michael; trainer, Brice Michael.

$2 Pick Three (3–1–5) Paid $189.00; Pick Three Pool $60,300.

81

2. **Fractional Times:** *DRF Simulcast Weekly* Official Charts contain every split time recorded in hundredths of a second. This is not available in the past performances found in *Daily Racing Form* or a track program. The Official Charts allow the handicapper to compare fractional times of like races conducted on a typical race card or race week.

FIFTH RACE
Aqueduct
DECEMBER 13, 2002

6 FURLONGS. (Inner Dirt)(1.08²) CLAIMING. Purse $16,000. For Fillies Three Years Old. Weight 122 lbs. Non-winners of two races since October 18 allowed, 1 lbs. A race since then, 3 lbs. CLAIMING PRICE $16,000, for each $2,000 to $14,000 2 lbs. (Races where entered for $12,500 or less not considered). (Registered New York Breds allowed 3 lbs.).

Value of Race: $16,000 Winner $9,600; second $3,200; third $1,760; fourth $960; fifth $480.   Mutuel Pool $317,819.00 Exacta Pool $315,603.00 Trifecta Pool $208,746.00

Last Raced	Horse	M/Eqt. A.Wt	PP St	¼	½	Str Fin	Jockey	Cl'g Pr	Odds $1
8Aug02 9Sar9	Queen Of Saratoga	Lb 3 116	6 2	2hd	31	1hd 1½	Lopez C C	14000	9.90
22Nov02 1Aqu4	O'cesadorable	L 3 116	8 8	91	6hd	5hd 2½	Luzzi M J	16000	13.10
22Nov02 1Aqu6	Sunshine Dreamer	L 3 12⁴	7 10	6hd	4hd	4½ 33	Nelson D	16000	10.30
23Oct02 1Aqu8	Jill Rabbit	Lf 3 116	3 3	31	1hd	21 4hd	Juarez A J Jr	14000	3.65
18Nov02 4Med2	Nice Little Girl	f 3 110	5 4	1hd	2hd	3hd 5nk	Ramos H G5	14000	15.90
9Nov02 4Del5	Pure Wild	Lb 3 116	9 6	5hd	7hd	73 61	Bridgmohan S X	16000	15.70
14Nov02 4Aqu7	Sea Of Hope	L 3 116	1 7	4½	5½	6½ 74¾	Toscano P R	16000	57.00
22Nov02 1Aqu3	Sunset Express	Lb 3 119	11 1	7hd	83	8½ 8½	Gryder A T	16000	2.65
24Nov02 2Aqu6	Thisililgirlcanrun	Lb 3 119	4 9	11	102	102 9½	Migliore R	16000	a-2.55
15Mar02 1Aqu1	Sweep North	Lb 3 114	2 11	102	102	9hd103¾	Chavez Luis5	16000	a-2.55
13Sep02 5Bel8	Butterfly Dancer	Lb 3 119	10 5	81	9½	11 11	Rojas R I	16000	97.00

a-Coupled: Thisililgirlcanrun and Sweep North.

OFF AT 2:21 Start Good. Won driving. Track fast.
TIME :23, :46⁴, :59, 1:11⁴ (:23.28, :46.88, :59.14, 1:11.93)

$2 Mutuel Prices:	5-QUEEN OF SARATOGA	21.80	13.00	7.50
	7-O'DESADORABLE		15.40	9.20
	6-SUNSHINE DREAMER			6.40

$2 EXACTA 5-7 PAID $3'0.00 $2 TRIFECTA 5-7-6 PAID $2,073.00

B. f., (Mar), by Signal Tap-Superetta, by Saratoga Six. Trainer Parisella John. Bred by Questroyal Stud LLC & Gavin Murphy (NY).

QUEEN OF SARATOGA pressured the pace three wide, dueled from the top of the stretch, edged clear nearing the sixteenth pole then kept an edge under solid handling. O'DESADORABLE rated back off the rail, was eased out making her bid entering the stretch, got up for place late and was gaining. SUNSHINE DREAMER rated close off the rail, angled five wide making her bid from the quarter pole, closed well under a steady drive but was outfinished for place the final yards. JILL RABBIT led briefly early then pressured the pace from the inside, dueled briefly clear entering the stretch, stayed game to the sixteenth pole then reluctantly yielded. NICE LITTLE GIRL set a pressured pace from between rivals, dropped back entering the stretch and leveled out the final furlong. PURE WILD rated close toward the outside, was steadied trying to get out on the turn and finished evenly. SEA OF HOPE rated close inside, was off the rail through the turn and empty in the stretch. SUNSET EXPRESS chased the pace from the outside, was wicest on the turn and offered no rally. THISLIL GIRLCANRUN dropped back early. SWEEP NORTH showed no speed and offered no rally. BUTTERFLY DANCER chased the pace from the outside, steadied slightly nearing the turn then gave way.

Owners— 1, Kupferberg Saul J & Max; 2, Desacora Joan & Perderis Dimitri J; 3, C D & G Stable; 4, Team Valor Stables; 5, Stonehearted Chic Stables; 6, Rottkamp John R; 7, Stellar Stable; 8, Misa Robert W Jr; 9, For Tne Kids Stable Foss Monty & Mo; 10, Equispeed Stable; 11, Our Dream Stable

Trainers— 1, Parisella John; 2, Hough Stanley M; 3, Klesaris Rober: P; 4, Galluscio Dominic G; 5, Jerkens Steven T; 6, Klesaris Steve; 7, Nolan Donna; 8, Friedman Mitchell; 9, Contessa Gary C; 10, Contessa Gary C; 11, Cuadra Victor

Jill Rabbit was claimed by C D & G Stable; trainer, Klesaris Robert P.; Sea Of Hope was claimed by Mariano John; trainer, Contessa Gary C.; Sweep North was claimed by Brice Michael; trainer. Brice Michael.

$2 Pick Three (3-1-5) Faid $189.00; Pick Three Pool $60,300.

83

FIRST RACE

Aqueduct
DECEMBER 15, 2002

6 FURLONGS. (Inner Dirt)(1.08²) CLAIMING. Purse $11,000. For Three Year Olds And Upward. Three Year Olds 122 lbs.; Older 123 lbs. Non-winners of two races since November 2 allowed, 2 lbs. Two races since October 11, 4 lbs. A race since then, 6 lbs. CLAIMING PRICE $10,000. (Races where entered for $7,000 or less not considered). (Registered New York Breds allowed 3 lbs.). (Clear. 45.)

Value of Race: $11,000 Winner $6,600; second $2,200; third $1,210; fourth $660; fifth $330. Mutuel Pool $112,065.00
$190,676.00 Trifecta Pool $112,065.00   Mutuel Pool $173,139.00 Exacta Pool

Last Raced	Horse	M/Eqt. A.Wt	PP	St	¼	½	Str	Fin	Jockey	Cl'g Pr	Odds $1
10Nov02 1Aqu5	Rich Coins	Lbf 4 112	4	8	8¹	6¹	2²	14¾	McKee J5	10000	1.50
8Dec02 1Aqu10	Alex's Love	Lb 4 117	1	3	1½	1hd	1¹	2¹¾	Smith A E	10000	3.85
21Nov02 9Aqu10	Vincent De Paul	L 4 117	9	2	4¹	4²	5¹½	3½	Mojica R Jr	10000	24.00
12May02 5Del7	Hunt Gold	Lbf 4 117	5	5	3½	3hd	4½	4¹½	Velazquez D C	10000	3.55
23Nov02 9Aqu8	Polish Missile	Lbf 5 112	2	4	2½	2¹	3hd	5¹¾	Ramos H G5	10000	a-5.80
16Nov02 2Med7	Hope To Prosper	Lb 4 116	7	6	7¹½	8³	7²½	6¹	Morales Oscar	10000	74.50
7Sep02 9FL4	Gypsy Sparkle	Lb 7 114	6	1	5hd	5½	6¹	7¾	Arroyo N Jr	10000	7.10
21Nov02 2Med5	Red Shift	Lbf 5 117	3	1	9	9	9	8⁴	Rojas R I	10000	a-5.80
8Dec02 1Aqu9	Mhalik–CH	Lb 4 117	8	7	6¹	7hd	8¹	9	Persaud R	10000	53.50

a–Coupled: Polish Missile and Red Shift.

OFF AT 12:31 Start Good. Won driving. Track fast.
TIME :23, :46², :59¹, 1:11 (:23.14, :46.56, :59.34, 1:11.00)

$2 Mutuel Prices:
2B –RICH COINS	5.00	2.90	2.60
3 –ALEX'S LOVE		3.80	3.40
11 –VINCENT DE PAUL			6.80

$2 EXACTA 2–3 PAID $21.20 $2 TRIFECTA 2–3–11 PAID $220.00

Dk. b. or br. c, by Rizzi–Valid Coins, by Valid Appeal. Trainer Dutrow Richard E Jr. Bred by Mockingbird Farm, Inc. (Fla.).

RICH COINS was outrun early, circled the field moving six wide passing the quarter pole and won going away under energetic hand urging. ALEX'S LOVE set a pressured pace on the inside and came up second best. VINCENT DE PAUL chased the pace on the outside and weakened. HUNT GOLD chased inside and had no rally. POLISH MISSILE pressed the pace in the two path and tired in the stretch. HOPE TO PROSPER raced inside and made no bid. GYPSY SPARKLE failed to respond. RED SHIFT did not factor. MHALIK (CHI) raced three wide down the backside and faded.

Owners— 1, Goldfarb Sanford Hemlock Hills Rose; 2, Sirica & Stathis Stables; 3, Joscelyn Robert; 4, Casson Helen G & Lanzara Ed; 5, Manorwood Stables; 6, Bill O'Toole Stables; 7, Pont Street Stable; 8, Valenti Anthony & Otto Phil Farms; 9, Calabrese Anthony

Trainers—1, Dutrow Richard E Jr; 2, Aquilino Joseph; 3, Barker Edward R; 4, Velazquez Alfredo; 5, Gullo Gary P; 6, Correa Jeff; 7, Carroll Del W II; 8, Gullo Gary P; 9, Lalman Dennis

Rich Coins was claimed by La Marca Stable; trainer, Servis Jason.
Scratched— Our Man (7Dec02 1AQU8), Poppy M (19Nov02 7MED3), Double Screen (27Nov02 2AQU4), River Raven (4Dec02 1AQU3)

3. **Positions with Margins:** The Official Charts detail horses' running positions at fractional call points and the margins ahead or behind at that particular time. Positioning and margins, combined with a footnote, give the handicapper a better visual of a race.

FIFTH RACE
Aqueduct
DECEMBER 13, 2002

6 FURLONGS. (Inner Dirt)(1.08²) CLAIMING. Purse $16,000. For Fillies Three Years Old. Weight 122 lbs. Non-winners of two races since October 18 allowed, 1 lbs. A race since then, 3 lbs. CLAIMING PRICE $16,000, for each $1,000 to $14,000 2 lbs. (Races where entered for $12,500 or less not considered). (Registered New York Breds allowed 3 lbs.).

Value of Race: $16,000 Winner $9,600; second $3,200; third $1,760; fourth $960; fifth $480. Mutuel Pool $317,819.00 Exacta Pool $315,603.00 Trifecta Pool $208,746.00

Last Raced	Horse	M/Eqt.	A.Wt	PP	St	1/4	1/2	Str	Fin	Jockey	Cl'g Pr	Odds $1
8Aug02 9Sar⁹	Queen Of Saratoga	Lb	3 114	6	2	2hd	3¹	1hd	1½	Lopez C C	14000	9.90
22Nov02 1Aqu⁴	O'desadorable	L	3 119	8	8	9¹	6hd	5hd	2½	Luzzi M J	16000	13.10
22Nov02 1Aqu⁶	Sunshine Dreamer	L	3 121	7	10	6hd	4hd	4¹½	33	Nelson D	16000	10.30
23Oct02 1Aqu⁸	Jill Rabbit	Lf	3 115	3	3	3¹	1hd	2¹	4hd	Juarez A J Jr	14000	3.65
18Nov02 4Med²	Nice Little Girl	f	3 110	5	4	1hd	2hd	3hd	5nk	Ramos H G⁵	14000	15.90
9Nov02 4Del⁵	Pure Wild	Lb	3 119	9	6	5hd	7hd	73	6¹	Bridgmohan S X	16000	15.70
14Nov02 4Aqu⁷	Sea Of Hope	L	3 116	1	7	4½	5½	6¹½	7¼½	Toscano P R	16000	57.00
22Nov02 1Aqu³	Sunset Express	Lb	3 119	11	1	7hd	83	8½	8½	Gryder A T	16000	2.65
24Nov02 2Aqu⁶	Thisliligirlcanrun	Lb	3 119	4	9	11	11	102	9¾	Migliore R	16000	a-2.55
15Mar02 1Aqu¹	Sweep North	Lb	3 114	2	11	102	102	9hd	10³¾	Chavez Luis⁵	16000	a-2.55
13Sep02 5Bel⁸	Butterfly Dancer	Lb	3 119	10	5	8¹	9½	11	11	Rojas R I	16000	97.00

a-Coupled: Thisliligirlcanrun and Sweep North.

OFF AT 2:21 Start Good. Won driving. Track fast.
TIME :23¹, :46⁴, :59, 1:11⁴ (:23.28, :46.88, :59.14, 1:11.93)

$2 Mutuel Prices:

5-QUEEN OF SARATOGA	21.80	13.00	7.50
7-O'DESADORABLE		15.40	9.20
6-SUNSHINE DREAMER			6.40

$2 EXACTA 5-7 PAID $310.00 $2 TRIFECTA 5-7-6 PAID $2,073.00

B. f, (Mar), by Signal Tap-Superetta, by Saratoga Six. Trainer Parisella John. Bred by Questroyal Stud LLC & Gavin Murphy (NY).

QUEEN OF SARATOGA pressured the pace three wide, dueled from the top of the stretch, edged clear nearing the sixteenth pole then kept an edge under solid handling. O'DESADORABLE rated back off the rail, was eased out making her bid entering the stretch, got up for place late and was gaining. SUNSHINE DREAMER rated close off the rail, angled five wide making her bid from the quarter pole, closed well under a steady drive but was outfinished for place the final yards. JILL RABBIT led briefly early then pressured the pace from the inside, dueled briefly clear entering the stretch, stayed game to the sixteenth pole then reluctantly yielded. NICE LITTLE GIRL set a pressured pace from between rivals, dropped back entering the stretch and leveled out the final furlong. PURE WILD rated close toward the outside, was steadied trying to get out on the turn and finished evenly. SEA OF HOPE rated close inside, was off the rail through the turn and empty in the stretch. SUNSET EXPRESS chased the pace from the outside, was widest on the turn and offered no rally. THISLILGIRLCANRUN dropped back early. SWEEP NORTH showed no speed and offered no rally. BUTTERFLY DANCER chased the pace from the outside, steadied slightly nearing the turn then gave way.

Owners— 1, Kupferberg Saul J & Max; 2, Desadora Joan & Perdaris Dimitri; 3, C D & G Stable; 4, Team Valor Stables; 5, Stonehearted Chic Stables; 6, Rottkamp John R; 7, Stellar Stable; 8, Misa Robert W Jr; 9, For The Kids Stable Foss Monty & Mo; 10, Equispeed Stable; 11, Our Dream Stable

Trainers— 1, Parisella John; 2, Hough Stanley M; 3, Klesaris Robert P; 4, Galluscio Dominic G; 5, Jerkens Steven T; 6, Klesaris Steve; 7, Nolan Donna; 8, Friedman Mitchell; 9, Contessa Gary C; 10, Contessa Gary C; 11, Cuadra Victor

Jill Rabbit was claimed by C D & G Stable; trainer, Klesaris Robert P.,
Sea Of Hope was claimed by Moirano Gerald & James; trainer, Contessa Gary C.,
Sweep North was claimed by Brice Michael; trainer, Brice Michael.

$2 Pick Three (3-1-5) Paid $189.00; Pick Three Pool $60,300.

FIRST RACE
Aqueduct
DECEMBER 15, 2002

6 FURLONGS. (Inner Dirt)(1.08²) CLAIMING. Purse $11,000. For Three Year Olds And Upward. Three Year Olds 122 lbs.; Older 123 lbs. Non-winners of two races since November 2 allowed, 2 lbs. Two races since October 11, 4 lbs. A race since then, 6 lbs. CLAIMING PRICE $10,000. (Races where entered for $7,000 or less not considered). (Registered New York Breds allowed 3 lbs.). (Clear. 45.)

Value of Race: $11,000 Winner $6,600; second $2,200; third $1,210; fourth $660; fifth $330. Mutuel Pool $173,139.00 Exacta Pool $190,676.00 Trifecta Pool $112,065.00

Last Raced	Horse	M/Eqt. A.Wt	PP	St	1/4	1/2	Str	Fin	Jockey	Cl'g Pr	Odds $1
10Nov02 1Aqu5	Rich Coins	Lbf 4 112	4	8	8¹	6¹	2²	14¾	McKee J5	10000	1.50
8Dec02 1Aqu10	Alex's Love	Lb 4 117	1	3	1½	1hd	1¹	2¹¾	Smith A E	10000	3.85
21Nov02 9Aqu10	Vincent De Paul	L 4 117	9	2	4¹	4²	5¹½	3¾	Mojica R Jr	10000	24.00
12May02 5Del7	Hunt Gold	Lbf 4 117	5	5	3½	3hd	4¹	4¹½	Velazquez D C	10000	3.55
23Nov02 9Aqu8	Polish Missile	Lbf 5 112	2	4	2½	2¹	3hd	5¹¾	Ramos H G5	10000	a-5.80
16Nov02 2Med7	Hope To Prosper	Lb 4 116	7	6	7¹½	8³	7²½	6¹	Morales Oscar	10000	74.50
7Sep02 9FL4	Gypsy Sparkle	Lb 7 114	6	1	5hd	5¹	6¹	7¾	Arroyo N Jr	10000	7.10
21Nov02 2Med5	Red Shift	Lbf 5 117	3	9	9	9	9	8⁴	Rojas R I	10000	a-5.80
8Dec02 1Aqu9	Mhalik-CH	Lb 4 117	8	7	6¹	7hd	3¹	9	Persaud R	10000	53.50

a–Coupled: Polish Missile and Red Shift.

OFF AT 12:31 Start Good. Won driving. Track fast.
TIME :23, :46², :59¹, 1:11 (:23.14, :46.56, :59.34, 1:11.00)

$2 Mutuel Prices:

2B –RICH COINS	5.00	2.90	2.60
3 –ALEX'S LOVE		2.90	3.40
11 –VINCENT DE PAUL			6.80

$2 EXACTA 2–3 PAID $21.20 $2 TRIFECTA 2–3–11 PAID $220.00

Dk. b. or br. c, by Rizzi–Valid Coins, by Valid Appeal. Trainer Dutrow Richard E Jr. Bred by Mockingbird Farm, Inc. (Fla).

RICH COINS was outrun early, circled the field moving six wide passing the quarter pole and won going away under energetic hand urging. ALEX'S LOVE set a pressured pace on the inside and came up second best. VINCENT DE PAUL chased the pace on the outside and weakened. HUNT GOLD chased inside and had no rally. POLISH MISSILE pressed the pace in the two path and tired in the stretch. HOPE TO PROSPER raced inside and made no bid. GYPSY SPARKLE failed to respond. RED SHIFT did not factor. MHALIK (CHI) raced three wide down the backside and faded.

Owners– 1, Goldfarb Sanford Hemlock Hills Rose; 2, S rica & Stathis Stables; 3, Joscelyn Robert; 4, Casson Helen G & Lanzara Ed; 5, Manorwood Stables; 6, Bill O'Toole Stable; 7, Pont Street Stable; 8, Valenti Anthony & Otto Phil Farms; 9, Calabrese Anthony

Trainers–1, Dutrow Richard E Jr; 2, Aquilino Joseph; 3, Barker Edward R; 4, Velazquez Alfredo; 5, Gullo Gary P; 6, Correa Jeff; 7, Carroll Del W II; 8, Gullo Gary P; 9, Lalman Dennis

Rich Coins was claimed by La Marca Stable; trainer, Servis Jason.
Scratched– Our Man (7Dec02 1AQU8), Poppy M (19Nov02 7MED3), Double Screen (27Nov02 2AQU4), River Raven (4Dec02 1AQU3)

4. **Key Races:** The Official Charts are a valuable tool to identify key races by circling horses who came back to win or place in their next race. Many handicappers use the Official Charts as archives and refer back to them many times during the handicapping process. (For expanded details on factoring in key races, please see Chapter 4.)

5. **Other Features:** The Official Charts document changes in track condition during a particular race day, detail race conditions, and report mutuel information.

FIFTH RACE
Aqueduct
DECEMBER 13, 2002

6 FURLONGS. (Inner Dirt) (1.082) CLAIMING. Purse $16,000. For Fillies Three Years Old. Weight 122 lbs. Non-winners of two races since October 18 allowed, 1 lbs. A race since then, 3 lbs. CLAIMING PRICE $16,000, for each $1,000 to $14,000 2 lbs. (Races where entered for $12,500 or less not considered).
(Registered New York Breds allowed 3 lbs.).

Value of Race: $16,000 Winner $9,600; second $3,200; third $1,760; fourth $960; fifth $480. Mutuel Pool $317,819.00 Exacta Pool $315,603.00 Trifecta Pool $208,746.00

Last Raced	Horse	M/Eqt. A.Wt	PP St	¼	½	Str Fin	Jockey	Cl'g Pr	Odds $1
8Aug02 9Sar9	Queen Of Saratoga	Lb 3 114	6 2	2hd	31	1hd 1½	Lopez C C	14000	9.90
22Nov02 1Aqu4	O'desadorable	L 3 119	8 8	91	5hd 2½	Luzzi M J	16000	13.10
22Nov02 1Aqu6	Sunshine Dreamer	L 3 121	7 10	6hd	4hd 41½ 33	Nelson D	16000	10.30
23Oct02 1Aqu8	Jill Rabbit	Lf 3 115	3 3	31	1hd 21 4hd	Juarez A J Jr	14000	3.65
18Nov02 4Med2	Nice Little Girl	Lb 3 110	5 4	1hd	2hd 3hd 5nk	Ramos H G5	14000	15.90
9Nov02 4Del5	Pure Wild	Lb 3 119	9 6	5hd	73 61	Bridgmohan S X	16000	15.70
14Nov02 4Aqu7	Sea Of Hope	L 3 116	1 7	4½	5½ 61½ 74¼	Toscano P R	16000	57.00
22Nov02 1Aqu3	Sunset Express	Lb 3 119	11 1	7hd	83 8½ 8½	Gryder A T	16000	2.65
24Nov02 2Aqu6	Thisliligirlcanrun	Lb 3 119	4 9	11	11 102 9½	Migliore R	16000	a-2.55
15Mar02 1Aqu1	Sweep North	Lb 3 114	2 11	102	102 9hd103¾	Chavez Luis5	16000	a-2.55
13Sep02 5Bel8	Butterfly Dancer	Lb 3 119	10 5	81	9½ 11 11	Rojas R I	16000	97.00

a—Coupled: Thisliligirlcanrun and Sweep North.

OFF AT 2:21 Start Good. Won driving. Track fast.
TIME :231, :464, :59, 1:114 (:23.28, :46.88, :59.14, 1:11.93)

$2 Mutuel Prices:	5—QUEEN OF SARATOGA	21.80	13.00	7.50
	7—O'DESADORABLE		15.40	9.20
	6—SUNSHINE DREAMER			6.40

$2 EXACTA 5–7 PAID $370.00 $2 TRIFECTA 5–7–6 PAID $2,073.00

B. f, (Mar), by Signal Tap-Superetta, by Saratoga Six. Trainer Parisella John. Bred by Questroyal Stud LLC & Gavin Murphy (NY).

QUEEN OF SARATOGA pressured the pace three wide, dueled from the top of the stretch, edged clear nearing the sixteenth pole then kept an edge under solid handling. O'DESADORABLE rated back off the rail, was eased out making her bid entering the stretch, got up for place late and was gaining. SUNSHINE DREAMER rated close off the rail, angled five wide making her bid from the quarter pole, closed well under a steady drive but was outfinished for place the final yards. JILL RABBIT led briefly early then pressured the pace from the inside, dueled briefly clear entering the stretch, stayed game to the sixteenth pole then reluctantly yielded. NICE LITTLE GIRL set a pressured pace from between rivals, dropped back entering the stretch and leveled out the final furlong. PURE WILD rated close toward the outside, was steadied trying to get out on the turn and finished evenly. SEA OF HOPE rated close inside, was off the rail through the turn and empty in the stretch. SUNSET EXPRESS chased the pace from the outside, was without the rail through the turn and offered no rally. THISLIL GIRLCANRUN dropped back early. SWEEP NORTH showed no speed and offered no rally. BUTTERFLY DANCER chased the pace from the outside, steadied slightly nearing the turn then gave way.

Owners— 1, Kupferberg Saul J & Max; 2, Desadora Joan & Perdaris Dimitri J; 3, C D & G Stable; 4, Team Valor Stables; 5, Stonehearted Chic Stables; 6, Rottkemp John R; 7, Stellar Stable; 3, Misa Robert W Jr; 9, For The Kids Stable Foss Monty & Mo; 10, Equispeed Stable; 11, Our Dream Stable

Trainers—1, Parisella John; 2, Hough Stanley M; 3, Klesaris Robert P; 4, Galluscio Dominic G; 5, Jerkens Steven T; 6, Klesaris Steve; 7, Nolan Donna; 8, Friedman Mitchell; 9, Contessa Gary C; 10, Contessa Gary C; 11, Cuadra Victor

Jill Rabbit was claimed by C D & G Stable; trainer, Klesaris Robert P.;
Sea Of Hope was claimed by Morano John; trainer, Contessa Gary C.;
Sweep North was claimed by Brice Michael; trainer, Brice Michael.

$2 Pick Three (3–1–5) Paid $189.00; Pick Three Pool $60,300.

FIRST RACE
Aqueduct
DECEMBER 15, 2002

6 FURLONGS. (Inner Dirt) (1.08²) CLAIMING. Purse $11,000. For Three Year Olds And Upward. Three Year Olds 122 lbs.; Older 123 lbs. Non-winners of two races since November 2 allowed, 2 lbs. Two races since October 11, 4 lbs. A race since then, 6 lbs. CLAIMING PRICE $10,000. (Races where entered for $7,000 or less not considered). (Registered New York Breds allowed 3 lbs.). (Clear. 45.)

Value of Race: $11,000 Winner $6,600; second $2,200; third $1,210; fourth $660; fifth $330. Mutuel Pool $173,139.00 Exacta Pool $190,676.00 Trifecta Pool $112,065.00

Last Raced	Horse	M/Eqt. A.Wt	PP	St	1/4	1/2	Str	Fin	Jockey	Cl'g Pr	Odds $1
10Nov02 1Aqu5	Rich Coins	Lbf 4 112	1	8	8¹	6¹	2²	1⁴¾	McKee J5	10000	1.50
8Dec02 1Aqu10	Alex's Love	Lb 4 117	3	3	1½	1hd	1¹	2¹½	Smith A E	10000	3.85
21Nov02 9Aqu10	Vincent De Paul	L 4 117	9	2	4¹	4²	5¹½	3¹½	Mojica R Jr	10000	24.00
12May02 5Del7	Hunt Gold	Lbf 4 117	5	5	3½	3hd	4½	4¹¹	Velazquez D C	10000	3.55
23Nov02 9Aqu8	Polish Missile	Lbf 5 112	7	4	2½	2¹	3hd	5¹½	Ramos H G5	10000	a-5.80
16Nov02 2Med7	Hope To Prosper	Lb 4 116	6	6	7¹½	8³	7²½	6¹	Morales Oscar	10000	74.50
7Sep02 9FL4	Gypsy Sparkle	Lb 7 114	4	7	5hd	5½	6¹	7¾	Arroyo N Jr	10000	7.10
21Nov02 2Med5	Red Shift	Lbf 5 117	8	9	9	9	9	8⁴	Rojas R I	10000	a-5.80
8Dec02 1Aqu9	Mhalik-CH	Lb 4 117	2	1	6¹	7hd	8¹	9	Persaud R	10000	53.50

a-Coupled: Polish Missile and Red Shift.

OFF AT 12:31 Start Good. Won driving. Track fast.
TIME :23, :46², :59¹, 1:11 (:23.14, :46.56, :59.34, 1:11.00)

$2 Mutuel Prices:

2B–RICH COINS	5.00	2.90	2.60
3–ALEX'S LOVE		3.80	3.40
11–VINCENT DE PAUL			6.80

$2 EXACTA 2-3 PAID $21.20 $2 TRIFECTA 2-3-11 PAID $220.00

Dk. b. or br. c, by Rizzi–Valid Coins, by Valid Appeal. Trainer Dutrow Richard E Jr. Bred by Mockingbird Farm, Inc. (Fla).

RICH COINS was outrun early, circled the field moving six wide passing the quarter pole and won going away under energetic hand urging. ALEX'S LOVE set a pressured pace on the inside and came up second best. VINCENT DE PAUL chased the pace on the outside and weakened. HUNT GOLD chased inside and had no rally. POLISH MISSILE pressed the pace in the two path and tired in the stretch. HOPE TO PROSPER raced inside and made no bid. GYPSY SPARKLE failed to respond. RED SHIFT did not factor. MHALIK (CHI) raced three wide down the backside and faded.

Owners—1, Goldfarb Sanford Hemlock Hills Rose; 2, Sirica & Stathis Stables; 3, Joscelyn Robert; 4, Casson Helen G & Lanzara Ed; 5, Manorwood Stables; 6, Bill O'Toole Stables; 7, Pont Street Stable; 8, Valenti Anthony & Otto Phil Farms; 9, Calabrese Anthony

Trainers—1, Dutrow Richard E Jr; 2, Aquilino Joseph; 3, Barker Edward R; 4, Velazquez Alfredo; 5, Gullo Gary P; 6, Correa Jeff; 7, Carroll Del W II; 8, Gullo Gary P; 9, Lalman Dennis

Rich Coins was claimed by La Marca Stable; trainer, Servis Jason.

Scratched—Our Man (7Dec02 1AQU8), Poppy M (19Nov02 7MED3), Double Screen (27Nov02 2AQU4), River Raven (4Dec02 1AQU3)

6. **Trainers, Jockeys, Owners and recent claims:** The Official Charts also include the trainers, owners, and assigned jockeys for each starter. At the bottom of the chart in claiming events, there is a footnote indicating what horses, if any, were claimed out of a particular race.

FIFTH RACE
Aqueduct
DECEMBER 13, 2002

6 FURLONGS. (Inner Dirt)(1.08²) CLAIMING. Purse $16,000. For Fillies Three Years Old. Weight 122 lbs. Non-winners of two races since October 18 allowed, 1 lbs. A race since then, 3 lbs. CLAIMING PRICE $16,000, for each $1,000 to $14,000 2 lbs. (Races where entered for $12,500 or less not considered).

(Registered New York Breds allowed 3 lbs.).

Value of Race: $16,000 Winner $9,600; second $3,200; third $1,760; fourth $960; fifth $480. Mutuel Pool $317,819.00 Exacta Pool $315,603.00 Trifecta Pool $208,746.00

Last Raced	Horse	M/Eqt. A.Wt	PP	St	1/4	1/2	Str	Fin	Jockey	Cl'g Pr	Odds $1
8Aug02 9Sar9	Queen Of Saratoga	Lb 3 114	6	2	2hd	31	1hd	1½	Lopez C C	14000	9.90
22Nov02 1Aqu4	O'desadorable	L 3 119	8	8	91	6hd	5hd	2½	Luzzi M J	16000	13.10
22Nov02 1Aqu6	Sunshine Dreamer	L 3 121	7	10	6hd	4hd	4 1½	33	Nelson D	16000	10.30
23Oct02 1Aqu8	Jill Rabbit	Lf 3 115	3	3	31	1hd	21	4hd	Juarez A J Jr	14000	3.65
18Nov02 4Med2	Nice Little Girl	f 3 110	5	4	1hd	2hd	3hd	5nk	Ramos H G5	14000	15.90
9Nov02 4Del5	Pure Wild	Lb 3 119	9	6	5hd	7hd	73	61	Bridgmohan S X	16000	15.70
14Nov02 4Aqu7	Sea Of Hope	L 3 116	1	7	4½	5 1½	6 1½	74½	Toscano P R	16000	57.00
22Nov02 1Aqu3	Sunset Express	Lb 3 119	11	1	7hd	83	8½	81	Gryder A T	16000	2.65
24Nov02 2Aqu6	Thislilgirlcanrun	Lb 3 119	4	9	11	11	102	9¼	Migliore R	16000	a-2.55
15Mar02 1Aqu1	Sweep North	Lb 3 114	2	11	102	102	9hd	10¾	Chavez Luis5	16000	a-2.55
13Sep02 5Bel8	Butterfly Dancer	Lb 3 119	10	5	81	9½	11	11	Rojas R I	16000	97.00

a-Coupled: Thislilgirlcanrun and Sweep North.

OFF AT 2:21 Start Good. Won driving. Track fast.
TIME :23¹, :46⁴, :59, 1:11⁴ (:23.28, :46.88, :59.14, 1:11.93)

$2 Mutuel Prices:

5-QUEEN OF SARATOGA	21.80	13.00	7.50
7-O'DESADORABLE		15.40	9.20
6-SUNSHINE DREAMER			6.40

$2 EXACTA 5-7 PAID $310.00 $2 TRIFECTA 5-7-6 PAID $2,073.00

B. f, (Mar), by Signal Tap-Superetta, by Saratoga Six. Trainer Parisella John. Bred by Questroyal Stud LLC & Gavin Murphy (NY).

QUEEN OF SARATOGA pressured the pace three wide, dueled from the top of the stretch, edged clear nearing the sixteenth pole then kept an edge under solid handling. O'DESADORABLE rated back off the rail, was eased out making her bid entering the stretch, got up for place late and was gaining. SUNSHINE DREAMER raced close off the rail, angled five wide making her bid from the quarter pole, closed well under a steady drive but was outfinished for place the final yards. JILL RABBIT led briefly early then pressured the pace from the inside, dueled briefly clear entering the stretch, stayed game to the sixteenth pole then reluctantly yielded. NICE LITTLE GIRL set a pressured pace from between rivals, dropped back entering the stretch and leveled out the final furlong. PURE WILD rated close toward the outside, was steadied trying to get out on the turn and finished evenly. SEA OF HOPE rated close inside, was off the rail through the turn and empty in the stretch. SUNSET EXPRESS chased the pace from the outside, was widest on the turn and offered no rally. THISLILGIRLCANRUN dropped back early. SWEEP NORTH showed no speed and offered no rally. BUTTERFLY DANCER chased the pace from the outside, steadied slightly nearing the turn then gave way.

Owners— 1, Kupferberg Saul J & Max; 2, Desadora Joan & Perdaris Dimitri; 3, C D & G Stable; 4, Team Valor Stables; 5, Stonehearted Chic Stables; 6, Rottkamp John R; 7, Stellar Stable; 8, Misa Robert W Jr; 9, For The Kids Stable Foss Monty & Mo; 10, Equispeed Stable; 11, Our Dream Stable

Trainers— 1, Parisella John; 2, Hough Stanley M; 3, Klesaris Robert P; 4, Galluscio Dominic G; 5, Jerkens Steven T; 6, Klesaris Steve; 7, Nolan Donna; 8, Friedman Mitchell; 9, Contessa Gary C; 10, Contessa Gary C; 11, Cuadra Victor

Jill Rabbit was claimed by C D & G Stable; trainer, Klesaris Robert P.;
Sea Of Hope was claimed by Moirano John; trainer, Contessa Gary C.,
Sweep North was claimed by Brice Michael; trainer, Brice Michael.

$2 Pick Three (3-1-5) Paid $189.00; Pick Three Pool $60,300.

FIRST RACE

Aqueduct

6 FURLONGS. (Inner Dirt)(1.08²) **CLAIMING.** Purse $11,000. For Three Year Olds And Upward. Three Year Olds 122 lbs.; Older 123 lbs. Non-winners of two races since November 2 allowed, 2 lbs. Two races since October 11, 4 lbs. A race since then, 6 lbs. **CLAIMING PRICE $10,000.** (Races where entered for $7,000 or less not considered). (Registered New York Breds allowed 3 lbs.). (Clear. 45.)

DECEMBER 15, 2002

Value of Race: $11,000 Winner $6,600; second $2,200; third $1,210; fourth $660; fifth $330.   Mutuel Pool $173,139.00 Exacta Pool $190,676.00 Trifecta Pool $112,065.00

Last Raced	Horse	M/Eqt. A.Wt	PP	St	¼	½	Str	Fin	Jockey	Cl'g Pr	Odds $1
10Nov02 1Aqu5	Rich Coins	Lbf 4 112	4	8	8¹	6¹	2²	14¾	McKee J5	10000	1.50
8Dec02 1Aqu10	Alex's Love	Lb 4 117	1	3	1½	1hd	11	21¾	Smith A E	10000	3.85
21Nov02 9Aqu10	Vincent De Paul	L 4 117	9	2	41	42	5½	3½	Mojica R Jr	10000	24.00
12May02 5Del7	Hunt Gold	Lbf 4 117	5	5	3½	3hd	4½	41½	Velazquez D C	10000	3.55
23Nov02 9Aqu8	Polish Missile	Lbf 5 116	2	4	2½	21	3hd	51¾	Ramos H G5	10000	a-5.80
16Nov02 2Med7	Hope To Prosper	Lb 4 116	7	6	71½	83	72¾	61	Morales Oscar	10000	74.50
7Sep02 9FL4	Gypsy Sparkle	Lb 7 114	6	1	5hd	5½	61	7¾	Arroyo N Jr	10000	7.10
21Nov02 2Med5	Red Shift	Lbf 5 117	3	9	9	9	9	84	Rojas R I	10000	a-5.80
8Dec02 1Aqu9	Mhalik–CH	Lb 4 117	8	7	6¹	7hd	8¹	9	Persaud R	10000	53.50

a–Coupled: Polish Missile and Red Shift.

OFF AT 12:31 Start Good. Won driving. Track fast.
TIME :23, :46², :59¹, 1:11 (:23.14, :45.56, :59.34, 1:11.00)

$2 Mutuel Prices:	2B–RICH COINS	5.00	2.90	2.60
	3–ALEX'S LOVE		3.80	3.40
	11–VINCENT DE PAUL			6.80

$2 EXACTA 2–3 PAID $21.20 $2 TRIFECTA 2–3–11 PAID $220.00

Dk. b. or br. c, by Rizzi–Valid Coins, by Valid Appeal. Trainer Dutrow Richard E Jr. Bred by Mockingbird Farm, Inc. (Fla.).

RICH COINS was outrun early, circled the field moving six wide passing the quarter pole and won going away under energetic hand urging. ALEX'S LOVE set a pressured pace on the inside and came up second best. VINCENT DE PAUL chased the pace on the outside and weakened. HUNT GOLD chased inside and had no rally. POLISH MISSILE pressed the pace in the two path and tired in the stretch. HOPE TO PROSPER raced inside and made no bid. GYPSY SPARKLE failed to respond. RED SHIFT did not factor. MHALIK (CHI) raced three wide down the backside and faded

Owners— 1, Goldfarb Sanford Hemlock Hills Rose; 2, Sirica & Stathis Stables; 3, Joscelyn Robert; 4, Casson Helen G & Lanzara Ed; 5, Manorwood Stables; 6, Bill O'Toole Stables; 7, Pont Street Stable; 8, Valenti Anthony & Otto Phil Farms; 9, Calabrese Anthony

Trainers— 1, Dutrow Richard E Jr; 2, Aquilino Joseph; 3, Barker Edward R; 4, Velazquez Alfredo; 5, Gullo Gary P; 6, Correa Jeff; 7, Carroll Del W II; 8, Gullo Gary P; 9, Lalman Dennis

Rich Coins was claimed by La Marca Stable; trainer, Servis Jason.

Scratched— Our Man (7Dec02 1AQU8), Poppy M (19Nov02 7MED3), Double Screen (27Nov02 2AQU4), River Raven (4Dec02 1AQU3)

15

THE WINNERS' BOOK

The Winners' Books listed in *DRF Simulcast Weekly* give the handicapper a concise snapshot of practically every race and every race card run in the country. By combining the Winners' Books, the complete race-result charts, and Beyer Pars, the player can sometimes uncover live longshots ready to give their best effort in their next start. These types of horses may have demonstrated some hidden sharp form, which may not have been easily noticeable using general past performances, and are likely to go unnoticed by the majority of the racing public, therefore offering great value at the betting windows. Here's a brief rundown on how the Winners' Books, when used in conjunction with racing charts, can be helpful in your daily handicapping routine.

1. **Convenient and Easy Reference:** The Winners' Book categories include date, race, track condition, type of race, distance, fractional times and final times (listed in hundredths), first three finishers and margins, winning style (see page 98), winning sire, winning Beyer Speed Figure, winning odds, and winning jockey and trainer. The handicapper, for example, can easily reference and compare the internal and final fractional times of two six-furlong $30,000 claiming races run the same day.

Date	Race	Cnd	Type of race	Dist	Fractions	Final	First three finishers (Margins)	Sty	Winning Sire	Beyer	Odds	Jockey	Trainer
12Dec21	1Aqu	gd	2 ⒻMd 30000	1m70y	:23.64 :48.64 1:15.50	1:47.24	Jacqueline E 2 Saint Brook ½ Raffie's Storm 4½	P	Honour and Glory	45	*1.55	Lopez C C	Barbara Robert
12Dec21	2Aqu		2 Clm 30000	6f	:23.51 :47.92 1:00.13	1:12.69	Ain't No... no Happy Trails 1¾ Subordinate's Lad 9¾	P	Northern Idol	69	8.00	Smith A E	Lalman Dennis
12Dec21	3Aqu	gd	2 ⒻMd 50000	6f	:22.96 :47.44 1:00.27	1:13.77	Phone No A Fam... nk Soul Of Solitude nk Haughty Lady 11¼	M	Favorite Trick	54	4.70	Migliore R	Contessa Gary C
12Dec21	4Aqu	gd	2 ⒮Md Sp Wt	1 1/16	:23.38 :48.57 1:15.14	1:47.88	Successful star 1 Cape Pogue 11½ Givemsilver hd	M	Mesopotamia	62	2.75	McKee J	Jerkens H Allen
12Dec21	5Aqu	gd	2 ⒻAw 44000n1x	1	:24.19 :48.36 1:14.04	1:39.43	Formal ...er 4¾ Rosie Is A Leader 18¼ Esb N' Flow ¾	P	Formal Gold	77	8.20	Bridgmohan S X	Donk David
12Dec21	6Aqu	gd	3 ↑ Md Sp Wt	6f	:23.49 :47.75 1:00.35	1:13.31	Wiseful 1 Gallorda 2¾ Bay Commander 2	P	Polish Numbers	75	6.10	Rojas R I	Jerkens H Allen
12Dec21	7Aqu	gd	3 ↑ Ⓕ⒮Aw 46000n2x	1m70y	:24.04 :48.55 1:14.44	1:43.55	Moor... and Beauty 5 Soon Soon 2¾ Safari Blues 1¼	P	Capote	78	3.15	Migliore R	Schosberg Richard
12Dec21	8Aqu	fst	3 ↑ ⒻAw 47000n3x	6f	:22.97 :46.22 :58.04	:09.93	Shankiri Miss 9 Ice Boots Baby 4¼ Marquee Kelly 3¼	P	Air Forbes Won	108	*0.75	McKee J	Reynolds Patrick L
12Dec21	9Aqu	fst	3 ↑ Clm 30000	6f	:23.61 :47.30 :59.66	1:12.47	Grade 1... Strike The Brass nk Master O Foxhounds nk	M	Prospectors Gamble	83	3.15	Luzzi M J	Levine Bruce N
13Dec21	1Aqu	fst	3 ↑ Ⓕ⒮Md Sp Wt	1 1/16	:23.71 :47.60 1:13.08	1:46.39	Michaelville 3½ Round On Ri 6¼ Dixie Dream 1½	C	Comet Shine	62	*1.70	Bridgmohan S X	Russo Sal
13Dec21	2Aqu	fst	3 ↑ Clm 12500	1 1/16	:23.95 :48.04 1:12.84	1:44.93	Langcara... me 2¾ Baby Sheq 2½ Nutforoveonmoney ½	P	Broad Brush	76	15.00	Rosado R J	Velazquez Alfredo
13Dec21	3Aqu	fst	3 ↑ ⒮Md Sp Wt	1 1/16	:23.86 :48.59 1:13.47	1:44.69	Indian Card 3½ Long Of The Mount 1½ Mister Fizz nk	P	Anziz	78	*0.65	Castellano J J	Jerkens James A
13Dec21	4Aqu	fst	3 ↑ ⒻMd Sp Wt	1m70y	:23.39 :47.78 1:12.35	1:43.57	Polish Gift 1 French Selection ¾ Conventionalwisdom 11½	M	Danzig	65	2.95	Castellano J J	McGaughey Claude III
13Dec21	5Aqu	fst	3 ⒻClm 16000	6f	:23.28 :45.88 :59.14	1:11.93	Queen C Seating ½ O'desadorable ½ Sunshine Dreamer 3	P	Signal Tap	66	9.90	Lopez C C	Parisella John
13Dec21	6Aqu	fst	2 Md Sp Wt	1m70y	:24.59 :49.10 1:13.94	1:42.52	Mustang Jack 5¾ Mumble Jumble 1¾ Casey's Bluff nk	P	Wild Again	81	2.95	Chavez Luis	McPeek Kenneth G
13Dec21	7Aqu	fst	3 ↑ ⒻAw 44000n2l	1 1/16	:23.92 :47.98 1:12.92	1:44.83	Grisham 4 Clear Destiny hd Charmer's Image ½	P	Grindstone	82	12.40	Castellano J J	Perkins Ben W Jr
13Dec21	8Aqu	fst	3 ↑ ⒻAw 48000n3x	1m70y	:24.52 :49.05 1:14.90	1:42.59	Ms. Rama... 3 I C Kiss 1¾ My Eloquent Miss 3¼	P	Whitney Tower	80	0.60	Luzzi M J	Levine Bruce N
13Dec21	9Aqu	fst	3 Clm 20000	1 1/16	:23.97 :47.78 1:13.49	1:44.13	Suave Devil 1½ Fine And Dandy 2¾ Wild Grose 2	P	Suave Prospect	89	*1.90	McKee J	Zito Nicholas P
14Dec21	1Aqu	sly	3 ⒻClm 25000	6f	:22.35 :46.37 1:00.06	1:14.79	When It Rains 5¾ You're On Your Own hd Ms. Amours 1¼	C	Salt Lake	60	19.20	Toscano P R	Disanto Glenn B
14Dec21	2Aqu	sly	3 ⒻMd Sp Wt	6f	:22.85 :46.55 :59.53	1:12.64	Miz Lynn... Kelly 3¾ Silver Debutante 1½ Ravish Me 2½	P	Langfuhr	79	2.50	Arroyo N Jr	Tesher Howard M
14Dec21	3Aqu	sly	2 ⒻMd 60000	1m70y	:23.91 :48.84 1:14.97	1:47.66	Lindeslady buck ½ Open And Shut 4¾ Her Place 2¾	P	Pembroke	60	7.30	Arroyo N Jr	Schettino Dominick A
14Dec21	4Aqu	sly	3 ⒻClm 60000	6f	:22.81 :46.41 :59.05	1:11.98	Gracious Assault 6 Lidbythedrop ¾ Cama's Dancer nk	C	Glitterman	83	6.30	Migliore R	Kimmel John C
14Dec21	5Aqu	sly	2 ⒻMd Sp Wt	1m70y	:23.46 :48.03 1:13.96	1:45.88	Show Dog nk Arabe Rose 3½ Three Roses ½	P	Holy Bull	64	5.20	Luzzi M J	Levine Bruce N
14Dec21	6Aqu	my	2 Ⓕ⒮Aw 43000n1x	6f	:22.77 :46.75 :59.19	1:12.29	Hansel Shielded ½ Storm On The Lake 2¾ Biggio's Beauty 1¾	P	Hansel	79	2.00	Pezua J M	Hertler John O
14Dec21	7Aqu	my	3 ↑ Aw 45000n2x	6f	:22.51 :45.50 :57.87	1:11.05	Pop Roc... 1¾ Lethal Weapon 2½ Conman Cunningham nk	P	Rocky Mountain	95	2.95	Chavez Luis	Lake Scott A
14Dec21	8Aqu	my	3 ↑ ⒻarlndRosesH75	6f	:22.41 :45.44 :57.31	1:10.10	Dat You wiz Blue 2¾ Xtra Heat 3¾ Belle Artiste 8¼	P	Cure the Blues	108	1.90	Velazquez J R	Jerkens James A
14Dec21	9Aqu	my	3 ↑ Clm 35000	1 1/16	:24.79 :49.37 1:14.25	1:46.21	Gail's Drive ✕ Bomboberegal 5¾ Hourly Storm 1¼	P	Ide	88	*2.35	Luzzi M J	Levine Bruce N

2. **How the Track Played:** The Winners' Book outlines in the "style" column the running style of the winner. Each winner is categorized as a pace (P), midpack (M), or come-from-behind (C) runner. The handicapper can determine if there was a trend regarding a particular day's races. For example, look at the Winners' Book for Aqueduct on December 14. On this particular day the track was labeled sloppy for the first five races, but was upgraded to muddy by the sixth race. The first three races produced winners that were come-from-behind runners indicated by the (C). As the track started to dry out during the afternoon, it started to favor horses racing on or close to the pace indicated by the (P). In fact, horses that were on or close to the lead won the last six races.

Date	Race	Cnd	Type of race	Dist	Fractions			Final	First three finishers (Margins)	Sty	Winning Sire	Beyer	Odds	Jockey	Trainer
14Dec02	1Aqu	sly	3 ⒻClm 25000	6f	:22.35	:46.37	1:00.06	1:14.79	**When It Rains ¾ You're On Your Own hd Ms. Amours 1¼**	C	**Salt Lake**	**60**	19.20	Toscano P R	Disanto Glenn B
14Dec02	2Aqu	sly	3↑ ⒻMd Sp Wt	6f	:22.85	:46.55	:59.53	1:12.64	**Miz Lynne Kelly 5¾ Silver Debutante 1½ Ravish Me 2½**	C	**Langfuhr**	**79**	2.50	Arroyo N Jr	Tesher Howard M
14Dec02	3Aqu	sly	2 ⒻMd 60000	1m70y	:23.91	:48.84	1:14.97	1:47.66	**Lindasladyluck 1 Open And Shut 4¾ Her Place 2¼**	C	**Pembroke**	**60**	7.30	Arroyo N Jr	Schettino Dominick A
14Dec02	4Aqu	sly	3 ⒻClm 60000	6f	:22.81	:46.41	:59.05	1:11.98	**Gracious Assault 5 Lifebythedrop ¾ Carrie's Dancer nk**	P	**Glitterman**	**83**	6.30	Migliore R	Kimmel John C
14Dec02	5Aqu	sly	2 ⒻMd Sp Wt	1m70y	:23.46	:48.03	1:13.96	1:45.38	**Show Bug nk Arctic Rose 3½ Three Roses ½**	P	**Holy Bull**	**64**	5.20	Luzzi M J	Levine Bruce N
14Dec02	6Aqu	my	2 ⒻⓈAlw 43000n1x	6f	:22.77	:46.75	:59.19	1:12.29	**Hansel's Crewel ½ Storm On The Lake 2½ Biagio's Beauty 1¾**	P	**Hansel**	**79**	2.00	Pezua J M	Hertler John O
14Dec02	7Aqu	my	3↑ Alw 45000n2x	6f	:22.51	:45.50	:57.87	1:11.05	**Pop Rocks 1¾ Lethal Weapon 2½ Conman Cunningham nk**	P	**Rocky Mountain**	**95**	2.95	Chavez Luis	Lake Scott A
14Dec02	8Aqu	my	3↑ ⒻGarlndRosesH75	6f	:22.41	:45.44	:57.31	1:10.10	**Dat You Miz Blue 2¼ Xtra Heat 5¾ Belle Artiste 8¼**	P	**Cure the Blues**	**108**	1.90	Velazquez J R	Jerkens James A
14Dec02	9Aqu	my	3↑ Clm 35000	$1\frac{1}{16}$	:24.79	:49.37	1:14.25	1:46.21	**Gail's Drive nk Berntoberegal 5¼ Hourly Storm 1¼**	P	**Ide**	**88**	*2.35	Luzzi M J	Levine Bruce N

3. **Beyer Pars:** The Winners' Book outlines Beyer Pars for every track. Beyer Pars are the typical Beyer Speed Figure that a horse would attain at that particular track and at a particular class level. For example, a horse winning at a claiming price of $35,000–$49,000 at Aqueduct would be expected to earn a Beyer Speed Figure of 92. Knowing the Beyer Par allows the handicapper to determine the overall strength of the race by comparing the race's winning Beyer with the Beyer Par.

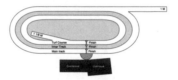

New York Racing Association Inc.,
Race Dates: Oct. 23-Dec. 31; Wednesday through Sunday
Takeout: 14% WPS; 20% Ex, DD, Q; 25% P3, P6, Tri, Super
N1X allow. purse: $43/44,000
MdSpWt purse: $41/42,000
Bottom claming: $14,000

BEYER PARS
3-Year-Olds and Up, Dirt

Condition	Par
Clm10000-14900	.80
Clm15000-20000	.84
Clm21000-34000	.89
NW2	.80
Clm35000-49000	.92
Clm50000-75000	.95
Clm75000 and up	.97
AlwN1X, N2L	.91
AlwN2X, N3L	.94
AlwN3X-N5X	.98

In the ninth race at Aqueduct on December 13, the winner, Suave Devil, earned an 89 Beyer Speed Figure for his victory in the $1\frac{1}{16}$-mile $20,000 claiming event. His 89 Beyer was five points higher than the Beyer Par for that class level (clm. 15,000–20,000: 84). This final race on the Aqueduct card was obviously an above-average group of $20K claimers, and the second- and third-place finishers (Fine And Dandy; Wild Goose) should be given extra consideration when returning to run at this same class level.

Date	Race	Cnd	Type of race	Dist	Fractions			Final	First three finishers (Margins)	Sty	Winning Sire	Beyer	Odds	Jockey	Trainer
13Dec02	1Aqu	fst	3 ↑ Ⓕ[S]Md Sp Wt	$1\frac{1}{16}$	:23.71	:47.60	1:13.08	1:46.39	**Michele Mel 3¼ Bound On Bi 6¼ Dixie Dream 1½**	C	**Comet Shine**	**62**	*1.70	Bridgmohan S X	Russo Sal
13Dec02	2Aqu	fst	3 ↑ Clm 12500	$1\frac{1}{16}$	:23.95	:48.04	1:12.84	1:44.93	**Largeandincharge 2¾ Baby Shaq 2½ Notforloveormoney ½**	P	**Broad Brush**	**76**	15.00	Rosado R J	Velazquez Alfredo
13Dec02	3Aqu	fst	3 ↑ [S]Md Sp Wt	$1\frac{1}{16}$	:23.86	:48.59	1:13.47	1:44.69	**Indian Card 5¼ King Of The Mount 1½ Mister Fizz** nk	P	**Anjiz**	**78**	*0.65	Castellano J J	Jerkens James A
13Dec02	4Aqu	fst	2 Md Sp Wt	1m70y	:23.39	:47.78	1:12.35	1:43.57	**Polish Gift 1 French Selection ¾ Conventionalwisdom 1½**	M	**Danzig**	**65**	2.95	Castellano J J	McGaughey Claude III
13Dec02	5Aqu	fst	3 ⒻClm 16000	6f	:23.28	:46.88	:59.14	1:11.93	**Queen Of Saratoga ½ O'desadorable ½ Sunshine Dreamer** 3	P	**Signal Tap**	**66**	9.90	Lopez C C	Parisella John
13Dec02	6Aqu	fst	2 Md Sp Wt	1m70y	:24.59	:49.10	1:13.94	1:42.52	**Mustang Jock 5¾ Mumble Jumble 1¾ Casey's Bluff** nk	P	**Wild Again**	**81**	2.95	Chavez Luis	McPeek Kenneth G
13Dec02	7Aqu	fst	3 ↑ ⒻAlw 44000n2l	$1\frac{1}{16}$	:23.92	:47.98	1:12.92	1:44.83	**Grisham ¾ Clear Destiny** hd **Charmer's Image ½**	P	**Grindstone**	**82**	12.40	Castellano J J	Perkins Ben W Jr
13Dec02	8Aqu	fst	3 ↑ ⒻAlw 48000n3x	1m70y	:24.52	:49.05	1:14.03	1:42.59	**Ms. Rapunzel 3 T C Kiss 1¾ My Eloquent Miss 3¼**	P	**Whitney Tower**	**80**	*0.60	Luzzi M J	Levine Bruce N
13Dec02	9Aqu	fst	3 Clm 20000	$1\frac{1}{16}$	:23.97	:48.78	1:13.49	1:44.13	**Suave Devil 1½ Fine And Dandy 2¾ Wild Goose** 2	P	**Suave Prospect**	**89**	*1.90	McKee J	Zito Nicholas P

NINTH RACE
Aqueduct
DECEMBER 13, 2002

1 1/16 MILES. (Inner Dirt)(1.41) CLAIMING. Purse $22,000. For Three Year Olds. Weight 123 lbs. Non–winners of two races at a mile or over since October 23 allowed, 1 lbs. Such a race since then, 3 lbs. CLAIMING PRICE $20,000, for each $1,000 to $18,000 2 lbs. (Races where entered for $16,000 or less not considered). (Registered New York Breds allowed 3 lbs.).

Value of Race: $22,000 Winner $13,200; second $4,400; third $2,420; fourth $1,320; fifth $660. Mutuel Pool $348,708.00 Exacta Pool $365,858.00 Trifecta Pool $266,433.00 Superfecta Pool $110,996.00

Last Raced	Horse	M/Eqt.	A.Wt	PP	St	¼	½	¾	Str	Fin	Jockey	Cl'g Pr	Odds $1
27Nov02 5Aqu3	Suave Devil	L	3 115	5	4	1½	1hd	1hd	11	11½	McKee J5	20000	1.90
1Dec02 2Aqu6	Fine And Dandy	Lbf	3 122	9	6	21	21	21½	21½	22¾	Migliore R	20000	5.20
27Nov02 5Aqu4	Wild Goose	L	3 120	8	5	5hd	6½	3½	33	32	Arroyo N Jr	20000	13.60
5Nov02 1Aqu6	Lilt	Lbf	3 114	11	8	7½	91½	7hd	52	4¾	Gryder A T	18000	16.00
6Dec02 1Aqu2	Coach Knight	Lb	3 116	4	1	3hd	5½	8hd	4hd	51½	Pimentel J	18000	5.00
9Feb02 4Aqu2	Migrating	Lbf	3 116	7	11	12	10hd	102	61½	61¼	Beckner D V	18000	8.70
9Nov02 1Aqu2	Mighty Gulch	L	3 120	3	12	11hd	12	113	8hd	72	Luzzi M J	20000	11.10
29Nov02 1Aqu6	Peruvian Summer	L	3 115	10	10	102	7½	5hd	7½	84¼	Chavez Luis5	20000	11.80
29Nov02 1Aqu10	Passionate Soldier	Lbf	3 120	6	3	4½	3hd	4hd	9hd	9nk	Lopez C C	20000	32.50
1Nov02 4Med6	Roy's Secret	Lbf	3 120	2	7	61	4hd	6½	103	103½	Whittaker D	20000	26.00
8Dec02 9Aqu11	Gleam Supreme		3 111	12	9	8hd	8hd	92	1110	1110¾	Ramos H G5	18000	108.50
5May02 5Aqu5	Cool Heavy Bull	Lb	3 120	1	2	9hd	111	12	12	12	Smith A E	20000	31.75

OFF AT 4:13 Start Good. Won driving. Track fast.
TIME :23^{4}, :48^{3}, 1:13^{2}, 1:37^{4}, 1:44 (:23.97, :48.78, 1:13.49, 1:37.84, 1:44.13)

$2 Mutuel Prices:				
	5–SUAVE DEVIL	5.80	4.50	3.50
	11–FINE AND DANDY		5.50	5.20
	10–WILD GOOSE			6.10

$2 EXACTA 5–11 PAID $43.00 $2 TRIFECTA 5–11–10 PAID $277.00 $2 SUPERFECTA 5–11–10–13 PAID $3,871.00

B. c, (May), by Suave Prospect–Carni Gal, by Carnivalay. Trainer Zito Nicholas P. Bred by William J Condren (Fla).

SUAVE DEVIL bobbled slightly at the start, rated the pace inside, was under pressure through the far turn then drew clear the final furlong. FINE AND DANDY rated with the pace in the three path, dueled through the upper stretch then yielded the final furlong. WILD GOOSE rated close toward the outside, made a four wide bid on the final turn and finished evenly. LILT rated off the pace toward the inside, angled out making his bid on the final turn, was six wide turning for home and leveled out in the drive. COACH KNIGHT rated close off the rail, made his bid through the final turn, was eased out for the drive and finished evenly. MIGRATING showed no speed, made a mild bid off the rail through the final turn, was eased out for the drive and finished evenly outside. MIGHTY GULCH raced unhurriedly saving ground and passed tiring rivals. PERUVIAN SUMMER kept just off the pace toward the outside, was widest through the final turn and empty in the stretch. PASSIONATE SOLDIER was kept close five and six wide then proved empty in the stretch. ROY'S SECRET rated close inside, gave chase into the final turn then gave way. GLEAM SUPREME, off the pace on the outside, tired eight wide on the final turn. COOL HEAVY BULL never factored.

Owners— 1, Condren William J; 2, Southern Stable; 3, Dubb Michael; 4, E L R Corp; 5, Riccio James et al; 6, Kupferberg Saul J & Max; 7, Sonny P Stable; 8, Carlucci Paul V & Singerman Martin; 9, Pugliese Savario; 10, Harris Myrna; 11, Marceda Michael; 12, Cirasola Salvatore & O'Rourke John

Trainers—1, Zito Nicholas P; 2, Lewis Lisa L; 3, Reynolds Patrick L; 4, Levine Bruce N; 5, Dutrow Richard E Jr; 6, Parisella John; 7, Martin Gregory F; 8, Destefano John M Jr; 9, Barker Edward R; 10, Schettino Dominick A; 11, Russo Sal; 12, Nevin Michael

Suave Devil was claimed by Team Jomar Stable; trainer, Martin Frank.,
Fine And Dandy was claimed by Jeronimo Mario; trainer, Petersen Dawn L.
Scratched— Stallvik (30Nov02 6MNR1), Chocolatemilksoup (15Nov02 5AQU7)

$2 Daily Double (4–5) Paid $10.40; Daily Double Pool $224,948.
$2 Pick Three (7–4–5) Paid $244.00; Pick Three Pool $104,121.
$2 Pick Four (2–7–4–5) Paid $1,980.00; Pick Four Pool $175,585.

Aqueduct Attendance: 2,939 Mutuel Pool: $710,287.00 ITW Mutuel Pool: $2,525,571.00 ISW Mutuel Pool: $5,157,701.00

4. **Internal and Final Fractions:** As mentioned earlier, the internal and final fractional times are listed in hundredths. These fractions assist the handicapper who makes his or her own pace and speed figures. (Please see Chapter 3, "Understanding Pace," for more information on making and evaluating pace figures.)

Date	Race	Cnd	Type of race	Dist	Fractions	Final	First three finishers (Margins)	Sty	Winning Sire	Beyer	Odds	Jockey	Trainer
12Dec02	1Aqu	gd	2 ⒻMd 30000	1m70y	23.64 .48.64 1:15.50	1:47.24	Jacqueline K 2 Saint Brook ½ Raffle's Storm 4½	P	Honour and Glory	45	*1.55	Lopez C C	Barbara Robert
12Dec02	2Aqu	gd	2 Clm 30000	6f	23.51 .47.92 1:00.13	1:12.69	Ain't No Sunshine no Happy Trails 1¾ Subordinate's Lad 9¾	P	Northern Idol	69	8.00	Smith A E	Lalman Dennis
12Dec02	3Aqu	gd	2 ⒻMd 50000	6f	22.96 .47.44 1:00.27	1:13.77	Phone Me A Favor nk Soul Of Solitude nk Haughty Lady 1¼	M	Favorite Trick	54	4.70	Miglore R	Contessa Gary C
12Dec02	4Aqu	gd	2 ⒮Md 50000	1¹⁄₁₆	23.38 .48.57 1:15.14	1:47.88	Success Minister 1 Cape Pogue 11½ Givensilver hd	M	Mesopotamia	62	2.75	McKee J	Jerkens H Allen
12Dec02	5Aqu	gd	2 ⒻAlw 44000n1x	1	24.19 .48.36 1:14.04	1:39.48	Formal Dancer 6¼ Rosie Is A Leader 18¼ Ebn N' Flow ¾	P	Formal Gold	77	8.20	Bridgmohan S X	Donk David
12Dec02	6Aqu	gd	3 ↑ Md Sp Wt	6f	23.49 .47.75 1:00.35	1:13.31	Wisenup 1 Golconda 2¾ Bay Commander 2	P	Polish Numbers	75	6.10	Rojas R	Jerkens H Allen
12Dec02	7Aqu	gd	3 ↑ ⒺⓈAw 46000n2x	1m70y	24.04 .48.55 1:14.44	1:43.55	Moonlighandbeauty 5 Soon Soon 2¾ Solar Blues 1¼	P	Capote	78	3.15	Miglore R	Schosberg Richard
12Dec02	8Aqu	fst	3 ↑ ⒻAlw 47000n3x	6f	22.97 .46.22 .58.04	1:09.93	Shawkiit Mint 9 Nice Boots Baby 4¼ Marquee Kelly 8¼	P	Air Forbes Won	108	*0.75	McKee J	Reynolds Patrick L
12Dec02	9Aqu	fst	3 ↑ Clm 30000	6f	22.61 .47.30 .59.66	1:12.47	Grady 1¼ Strike The Brass hd Master D Foxhounds nk	M	Prospectors Gamble	83	3.15	Luzzi M J	Levine Bruce N
13Dec02	1Aqu	fst	3 ↑ ⒺⓈMd Sp Wt	1¹⁄₁₆	23.71 .47.60 1:13.08	1:46.39	Michele Med 3¾ Bound On Bi 6¼ Dixie Dream 1½	C	Comet Shine	62	*1.70	Bridgmohan S X	Russo Sal
13Dec02	2Aqu	fst	3 ↑ Clm 12500	1¹⁄₁₆	23.35 .48.04 1:12.84	1:44.93	Largeandincharge 2¾ Baby Shaq 2½ Notforlovermoney ½	C	Broad Brush	76	15.00	Rosato R J	Velazquez Alfredo
13Dec02	3Aqu	fst	3 ↑ ⒮Md Sp Wt	1¹⁄₁₆	22.86 .48.59 1:13.47	1:44.69	Indian Card 5¼ King Of The Mount 1½ Mister Fizz nk	M	Anjiz	78	*0.65	Castellano J J	Jerkens James A
13Dec02	4Aqu	fst	3 Md Sp Wt	1m70y	23.39 .47.78 1:12.35	1:43.57	Polish Gift 1 French Selection ¾ Conventionalwisdom 1½	M	Danzig	65	2.95	Castellano J J	McGaughey Claude III
13Dec02	5Aqu	fst	3 ⒻClm 16000	6f	23.28 .46.88 .59.14	1:11.93	Queen Of Saratoga ½ O'desadorable ½ Sunshine Dreamer 3	P	Signal Tap	66	9.90	Lopez C C	Parisella John
13Dec02	6Aqu	fst	2 Md Sp Wt	6f	24.59 .49.10 1:13.94	1:42.52	Mustang Jock 5¾ Mumble Jumble 1¾ Casey's Bluff nk	P	Wild Again	81	2.95	Chavez Luis	McPeek Kenneth G
13Dec02	7Aqu	fst	3 ↑ ⒻAlw 44000n2l	1¹⁄₁₆	23.92 .47.98 1:12.92	1:44.83	Grisham ¾ Clear Destiny hd Charmer's Image ½	P	Grindstone	82	12.40	Castellano J J	Perkins Ben W Jr
13Dec02	8Aqu	fst	3 ↑ ⒻAlw 48000n3x	1m70y	24.52 .49.05 1:14.03	1:42.59	Ms. Rapunzel 3 T C Kiss 1¾ My Eloquent Miss 3¼	P	Whitney Tower	80	*0.60	Luzzi M J	Levine Bruce N
13Dec02	9Aqu	fst	3 Clm 20000	1¹⁄₁₆	23.97 .48.78 1:13.49	1:44.13	Suave Devil 1½ Fine And Dandy 2¾ Wild Goose 2	P	Suave Prospect	89	*1.90	McKee J	Zito Nicholas P
14Dec02	1Aqu	sly	3 ⒻClm 25000	6f	22.35 .46.37 1:00.06	1:14.79	When It Rains ¾ You're On Your Own 1hd Ms. Amours 1¼	C	Salt Lake	60	19.20	Toscano P R	Disanto Glenn B
14Dec02	2Aqu	sly	3 ↑ ⒻMd Sp Wt	6f	22.85 .46.55 .59.53	1:12.64	Miz Lynne Kelly 5¾ Silver Debutante 1½ Ravish Me 2½	C	Langfuhr	79	2.50	Arroyo N Jr	Tesher Howard M
14Dec02	3Aqu	sly	3 ⒻClm 60000	1m70y	23.91 .48.84 1:14.97	1:47.66	Lindasladyluck 1 Open And Shut 4¾ Her Place 2¾	C	Pembroke	60	7.30	Arroyo N Jr	Schettino Dominick A
14Dec02	4Aqu	sly	3 ⒻClm 60000	6f	22.81 .46.41 .59.05	1:11.98	Gracious Assault 5 Litebythedrop ¾ Camie's Dancer nk	P	Glitterman	83	6.30	Miglore R	Kimmel John C
14Dec02	5Aqu	sly	2 ⒻMd Sp Wt	1m70y	23.46 .48.03 1:13.96	1:45.88	Show Bug nk Arctic Rose 3½ Three Roses ½	P	Holy Bull	64	5.20	Luzzi M J	Levine Bruce N
14Dec02	6Aqu	my	2 ⒺⓈAlw 43000n1x	6f	22.77 .46.75 .59.19	1:12.29	Hansel's Gretel ½ Storm On The Lake 2¼ Bioglo's Beauty 1¾	P	Hansel	79	2.00	Pezua J M	Hertler John O
14Dec02	7Aqu	my	3 ↑ Alw 45000n2x	6f	22.51 .45.50 .57.87	1:11.05	Pop Rocks 1¼ Lethal Weapon 2½ Conman Cunningham nk	P	Rocky Mountain	95	2.95	Chavez Luis	Lake Scott A
14Dec02	8Aqu	my	3 ↑ ⒻⓈarlndRosesH75	6f	22.41 .45.44 .57.31	1:10.10	Dat You Miz Blue 2¼ Xtra Heat 5¾ Belle Artiste 8¼	P	Cure the Blues	108	1.90	Velazquez J R	Jerkens James A
14Dec02	9Aqu	my	3 ↑ Clm 35000	1¹⁄₁₆	24.79 .49.37 1:14.25	1:46.21	Gail's Drive nk Bomtoberegal 5¼ Hourly Storm 1¼	P	Ide	88	*2.35	Luzzi M J	Levine Bruce N

5. **Trainers and Jockeys:** The Winners' Book reports the winning jockey and trainer for each race. Players can track who is hot along with winning jockey-trainer combinations. For example, the Winners' Book was able to isolate the hot jockey-trainer combination of Mike Luzzi and Bruce Levine from December 12–14 at Aqueduct. As you can see, this duo teamed up to win four races in three days.

Date	Race	Cnd	Type of race	Dist	Fractions	Final	First three finishers (Margins)	Sty	Winning Sire	Beyer	Odds	Jockey	Trainer
12Dec02 1Aqu		gd	2 (F)Md 30000	1m70y	23.64 .48.64 1:15.50	1:47.24	Jacqueline K 2 Saint Brook ½ Raffie's Storm 4½	P	Honour and Glory	45	*1.55	Lopez C C	Barbara Robert
12Dec02 2Aqu		gd	2 Clm 30000	6f	23.51 .47.92 1:00.13	1:12.69	Ain't No Sunshine no Happy Trails 1¾ Subordinate's Lad 9¾		Northern Idol	69	8.00	Smith A E	Lalman Dennis
12Dec02 3Aqu		gd	2 (F)Md 50000	6f	22.96 .47.44 1:00.27	1:13.77	Phone Me A Favor nk Soul Of Solitude nk Haughty Lady 1¼	M	Favorite Trick	54	4.70	Migliore R	Contessa Gary C
12Dec02 4Aqu		gd	2 (S)Md Sp Wt	1 1/16	23.38 .48.57 1:15.14	1:47.88	Success Minister 1 Cape Pogue 11¼ Givensilver hd	M	Mesopotamia	62	2.75	McKee J	Jerkens H Allen
12Dec02 5Aqu		gd	2 (F)Alw 44000n1x	1	24.19 .48.36 1:14.04	1:39.48	Formal Dancer 6¼ Rosie Is A Leader 18¼ Ebb N' Flow ¾	M	Formal Gold	77	8.20	Bridgmohan S X	Dronk David
12Dec02 6Aqu		gd	3 + Md Sp Wt	6f	23.49 .47.75 1:00.35	1:13.31	Wisenup 1 Golconda 2¾ Bay Commander 2	P	Polish Numbers	75	6.10	Rojas R I	Jerkens H Allen
12Dec02 7Aqu		gd	3 + (F)(S)Alw 46000n2x	1m70y	24.04 .48.55 1:14.44	1:43.55	Moonlighthandbeauty 5 Soon Soon 2¾ Solar Blues 1¼	P	Cozzie	78	3.15	Migliore R	Schosberg Richard
12Dec02 8Aqu		fst	3 + (F)Alw 47000n3x	6f	22.97 .46.22 58.04	1:09.93	Shawdit Mint 9 Nice Boots Baby 1½ Marquee Kelly 8¼		Air Forbes Won	108	*0.75	McKee J	Reynolds Patrick L
12Dec02 9Aqu		fst	3 + Clm 30000	6f	23.61 .47.30 59.66	1:12.47	Grady 1½ Strike The Brass nk Master 0 Foxhounds nk	M	Prospectors Gamble	83	3.15	Luzzi M J	Levine Bruce N
30Dec02 1Aqu		fst	3 + (F)(S)Md Sp Wt	1 1/16	23.71 .47.60 1:13.08	:46.39	Michele Mel 3¾ Bourrf On BI 6¼ Dixie Dream 1½	C	Comet Shine	62	*1.70	Bridgmohan S X	Russo Sal
30Dec02 2Aqu		fst	3 + Clm 12500	1 1/16	23.95 .48.04 1:12.84	:44.93	Largeandincharge 2¾ Baby Shaq 2½ Notforlovoemoney ½	C	Broad Brush	76	15.00	Rosado R J	Velazquez Alfredo
30Dec02 3Aqu		fst	3 + (S)Md Sp Wt	1 1/16	23.86 .48.59 1:13.47	:44.69	Indian Card 5¼ King Of The Mount 1½ Mister Fizz nk	M	Anjiz	78	*0.65	Castellano J J	Jerkens James A
30Dec02 4Aqu		fst	2 Md Sp Wt	1m70y	23.39 .47.78 1:12.35	:43.57	Polish Gift 1 French Selection ¾ Conventionalwisdom 1½	M	Danzig	65	2.95	Castellano J J	McGaughey Claude III
30Dec02 5Aqu		fst	3 (F)Clm 16000	6f	23.28 .46.88 59.14	1:11.93	Queen Of Saratoga ½ 0'desadorable ½ Sunshine Dreamer 3	P	Signal Tap	66	9.90	Lopez C C	Parisella John
30Dec02 6Aqu		fst	2 Md Sp Wt		24.59 .49.10 1:13.94	1:42.52	Mustang Jock 5¾ Mumble Jumble 1¾ Casey's Bluff nk	P	Wild Again	81	2.95	Chavez Luis	McPeek Kenneth G
30Dec02 7Aqu		fst	3 + (F)Alw 44000n2l	1 1/16	23.92 .47.98 1:12.92	1:44.83	Grisham ¾ Clear Destiny hd Charmer's Image ½	P	Grindstone	82	12.40	Castellano J J	Perkins Ben W Jr
30Dec02 8Aqu		fst	3 + (F)Alw 48000n3x	1m70y	24.52 .49.05 1:14.03	1:42.59	Ms. Rapunzel 3 T C Kiss 1¾ My Eloquent Miss 3¼	P	Whitney Tower	80	*0.60	Luzzi M J	Levine Bruce N
30Dec02 9Aqu		fst	3 Clm 20000	1 1/16	23.97 .48.78 1:13.49	1:14.13	Suave Devil 1½ Fine And Dandy 2¾ Wild Goose 2	P	Suave Prospect	89	*1.90	McKee J	Zito Nicholas P
14Dec02 1Aqu		sly	3 + (F)Clm 25000	6f	22.35 .46.37 1:00.06	1:14.79	When It Rains ¾ You're On Your Own hd Ms. Amours 1¼	C	Salt Lake	60	19.20	Toscano P R	Disanto Glenn B
14Dec02 2Aqu		sly	3 + (F)Md Sp Wt	6f	22.85 .46.55 59.53	1:12.64	Miz Lynne Kelly 5¾ Silver Debutante 1½ Ravish Me 2½	C	Langfuhr	79	2.50	Arroyo N Jr	Tesher Howard M
14Dec02 3Aqu		sly	3 (F)Clm 60000	1m70y	23.91 .48.84 1:14.97	1:47.66	Lindasladyluck 1 Open And Shut 4¾ Her Place 2¼	C	Pembroke	60	7.30	Arroyo N Jr	Schettino Dominick A
14Dec02 4Aqu		sly	3 (F)Clm 6000	6f	22.81 .46.41 59.05	1:11.98	Gracious Assault 5 Litebythedrop ¾ Carrie's Dancer nk	C	Glitterman	83	6.30	Migliore R	Kimmel John C
14Dec02 5Aqu		sly	2 (F)Md Sp Wt	1m70y	23.46 .48.03 1:13.96	1:45.88	Show Bug nk Arctic Rose 3¼ Three Roses ½	P	Holy Bull	64	5.20	Luzzi M J	Levine Bruce N
14Dec02 6Aqu		my	3 + (F)(S)Alw 43000n1x	6f	22.77 .46.75 59.19	1:12.29	Hansel's Gretel ½ Storm On The Lake 2¼ Biogio's Beauty 1¾	P	Hansel	79	2.00	Pezua J M	Herttler John O
14Dec02 7Aqu		my	3 + (F)Alw 45000n2x	6f	22.51 .45.50 57.87	1:11.05	Pop Rocks 1¼ Lethal Weapon 2½ Conman Cunningham nk	P	Rocky Mountain	95	2.95	Chavez Luis	Lake Scott A
14Dec02 8Aqu		my	3 + (F)(S)arlndRosebH75	6f	22.41 .45.44 57.31	1:10.10	Dat You Miz Blue 2¾ Xtra Heat 5¾ Belle Artiste 8¼	P	Cure the Blues	108	1.90	Velazquez J R	Jerkens James A
14Dec02 9Aqu		my	3 + Clm 35000	1 1/16	24.79 .49.37 1:14.25	1:46.21	Gail's Drive nk Bombtoberegal 5¼ Hourly Storm 1¼	P	Ide	88	*2.35	Luzzi M J	Levine Bruce N

NINTH RACE — Aqueduct

DECEMBER 12, 2002

6 FURLONGS. (Inner Dirt)(1.082) CLAIMING. Purse $27,000 (Up To $5,238 NYSBFOA) For Three Year Olds And Upward. Three Year Olds 122 lbs.; Older 123 lbs. Non-winners of two races since October 23 allowed 1 lb. A race since then, 3 lbs. CLAIMING PRICE $30,000, for each $2,500 to $25,000 2 lbs. (Races where entered for $20,000 or less not considered). (Registered New York Breds allowed 3 lbs.)

Value of Race: $27,000 Winner $16,200; second $5,400; third $2,970; fourth $1,620; fifth $810. Mutuel Pool $268,439.00 Exacta Pool $283,033.00 Trifecta Pool $106,933.00 Superfecta Pool $31,327.00

Last Raced	Horse	M/Eqt. A.Wt	PP	St	¼	½	¾	Str	Fin	Jockey	Cl'g Pr	Odds $1
16Nov02 5Aqu2	Grady	Lbf 7 120	3	9	9	8½	4hd	11½	Luzzi M J	30000	3.15
21Nov02 2Aqu4	Strike the Brass	L 5 117	8	2	3¹½	1½	1½	2nk	Lopez C C	30000	8.00
28Nov02 2Aqu6	Master O Foxhounds	Lf 7 120	5	7	6¹	6¹½	5¹	3nk	Bridgmohan S X	27500	3.05
28Nov02 2Aqu4	Love Less	Lbf 4 117	9	5	4hd	3¹	2hd	4½	Castellano J J	30000	2.85
27Nov02 2Aqu1	Milky Bar-CH	Lb 6 113	7	1	7¹½	2¹	3²	5¹¾	McKee J5	27500	6.70
30Nov02 3FL2	Bogart	Lb 5 119	4	8	7¹½	7²	6²	6⁴¾	Blake J L	30000	9.20
17Nov02 1Aqu1	Lord Of Ewhurst	Lbf 4 114	1	4	2hd	4¹	7hd	7¹½	Chavez Luis5	30000	41.00
7Nov02 9Aqu9	Assmar	Lb 4 120	6	6	5hd	5hd	8²½	8¹¹¾	Rojas R I	30000	32.75
24Nov02 8FL5	Tony And Shaye	Lbf 5 120	2	3	8½	9	9	9	Beckner D V	30000	29.50

OFF AT 4:14 Start Good. Won driving. Track fast.

TIME :233, :471, :593, 1:122 (:23.61, :47.30, :59.66, 1:12.47)

$2 Mutuel Prices:

4—GRADY		8.30	4.60	2.50
6—STRIKE THE BRASS			7.40	4.20
5—MASTER O FOXHOUNDS				2.90

$2 EXACTA 4-9 PAID $61.50 $2 TRIFECTA 4-9-6 PAID $543.00
SUPERFECTA 4-9-6-10 PAID $192.00 $2

B. g. by Prospectors Gamble-Petadear, by Subpet. Trainer Levine Bruce N. Bred by Hart Farm Inc (Fla).

GRADY raced unhurriedly through the backstretch, ran evenly three wide on the turn then rallied from the top of the stretch, came between horses late and was clear the final yards. STRIKE THE BRASS rated with the pace toward the outside, took over three wide on the turn, dueled to a clear lead then was outfinished the final yards. MASTER O FOXHOUNDS kept just off the pace toward the inside, angled five wide on the turn and closed well through the stretch. LOVE LESS raced just off the pace outside, was five wide on the turn and finished evenly. MILKY BAR (CHI) advanced between horsed taking the early lead, dropped back toward the inside nearing the quarter pole, remained close through the stretch but outfinished the final furlong. BOGART was kept off the pace inside and proved empty in the stretch. LORD OF EWHURST stayed with the pace inside then showed no response through the turn. ASSMAR chased the pace from mid track and proved empty six wide on the turn. TONY AND SHAYE showed no speed off the rail, angled out nearing the turn then offered no rally widest.

Owners— 1, Valente Rodd J; 2, Karakorum Farm; 3, Terracciano Neal; 4, Rosenberg Joan & Demas Joseph F; 5, Imperio Joseph; 6, Miller Thomas & Stix-N-Stones Stabl; 7, Romero Gabriel; 8, Piazza Giuseppina & One Pond Stable; 9, Marinos Jane E & Alex A

Trainers—1, Levine Bruce N; 2, Odintz Jeff; 3, Terracciano Neal; 4, Galluscio Dominic G; 5, Imperio Joseph; 6, O'Connor Stephen; 7, Cuadra Victor; 8, Sciacca Gary; 9, Lecesse Michael

Strike the Brass was claimed by Guerrera Melissa; trainer, Hushion Michael E.

Scratched— Unreal Madness (28Jly02 5FLAR9).

$2 Daily Double (1-4) Paid $12.20; Daily Double Pool $219,867.
$2 Pick Three (5-1-4) Paid $49.40; Pick Three Pool $86,511.
$2 Pick Four (9-5-1-4) Paid $439.00; Pick Four Pool $152,554.

Aqueduct Attendance: 2,762 Mutuel Pool: $642,780.00 ITW Mutuel Pool: $2,229,105.00 ISW Mutuel Pool: $4,321,530.00

EIGHTH RACE
Aqueduct
DECEMBER 13, 2002

1 MILE 70 YARDS. (Inner Dirt)(1.38¾) ALLOWANCE. Purse $48,000. (Up To $9,312 NYSBFOA) For Fillies and Mares Three Years Old And Upward Which Have Never Won Three Races Other Than Maiden, Claiming, Starter, Or Restricted Or Which Have Never Won Four Races. Three Year Olds 121 lbs.; Older 123 lbs. Non-winners of $30,000 at a mile or over since October 28 allowed, 2 lbs. A race at a mile or over since then, 4 lbs. (Races where entered for $65,000 or less not considered in allowances). (Registered New York Breds allowed 3 lbs.).

Value of Race: $48,000 Winner $28,800; second $9,600; third $5,280; fourth $2,880; fifth $1,440. Mutuel Pool $240,836.00 Exacta Pool $233,616.00 Trifecta Pool $151,111.00

Last Raced	Horse	M/Eqt. A.Wt	PP	St	¼	½	¾	Str	Fin	Jockey	Odds $1
29Nov02 4Aqu1	Ms. Rapunzel	L 4 123	4	3	3½	3hd	1hd	11	13	Luzzi M J	0.60
2Nov02 4Aqu4	T C Kiss	Lb 4 119	3	4	5½½	52½	4½	2hd	21½	Smith A E	6.30
14Nov02 8Aqu5	My Eloquent Miss	L 4 114	6	5	41	41	3hd	32½	33¾	McKee J5	4.10
22Nov02 5Aqu4	Chinsegut	L 4 119	1	6	6	6	6	41½	47	Bridgmohan S X	24.25
7Nov02 2Aqu4	Any Scoop	Lf 4 116	5	2	2½½	21½	21	52½	57	Lopez C C	5.90
23Nov02 7Aqu5	Keratoid's Chubbs	Lf 5 119	2	1	11	1hd	51	6	6	Rojas R I	33.75

OFF AT 3:44 Start Good. Won driving. Track fast.

TIME :24², :49, 1:14, 1:38³, 1:42² (:24.52, :49.05, 1:14.03, 1:38.62, 1:42.59)

$2 Mutuel Prices:

4-MS. RAPUNZEL	3.20	2.40	2.10
3-T C KISS		3.50	2.10
6-MY ELOQUENT MISS			2.10

$2 EXACTA 4-3 PAID $9.30 $2 TRIFECTA 4-3-6 PAID $23.80

Ch. f, by Whitney Tower-Hail a Princess, by Hail the Ruckus. Trainer Levine Bruce N. Bred by Norman Dellheim & Gary J Mesnick (Fla).

MS. RAPUNZEL rated close in the three path, was on even terms through the final turn, drew clear entering the stretch then gradually widened under an aggressive hand ride. T C KISS rated close toward the inside, was eased three wide making her bid into the final turn, raced close inside through the stretch and settled for second best. MY ELOQUENT MISS rated close in the four path, made her bid from the top of the stretch then leveled out the final furlong. CHINSEGUT was a step slow to start, raced unhurriedly inside, made a mild bid off the rail on the final turn, was eased out for the drive and finished evenly. ANY SCOOP rated with the pace, was tested inside through the final turn then had nothing left in the drive. KERATOID'S CHUBBS was clear early, raced with the pace through the backstretch then faded saving ground on the final turn.

Owners— 1, Four Drake Stable; 2, Seinfeld Barry & Dodson Elizabeth K; 3, Flail Andrew J; 4, Blue Stork Stables; 5, Moss Maggie; 6, Tiamfook Steve C

Trainers—1, Levine Bruce N; 2, Kappes Steven W; 3, Iwinski Allen; 4, Sedlacek Roy; 5, Contessa Gary C; 6, Tiamfook Steve C

$2 Pick Six (3-1-5-2-7-4) 5

Correct Paid $317.50; Pick Six Pool $69,116; Carryover Pool $41,469.

NINTH RACE
Aqueduct
DECEMBER 14, 2002

1$\frac{1}{16}$ MILES. (Inner Dirt)(1.41) CLAIMING. Purse $32,500. (Up To $6,305 NYSBFOA) For Three Year Olds And Upward. Three Year Olds 121 lbs.; Older 123 lbs. Non-winners of two races at a mile or over since October 22 allowed, 1 lbs. Such a race since then, 3 lbs. CLAIMING PRICE $35,000; for each $2,500 to $30,000, allowed 2 lbs. (Races where entered for $25,000 or less not considered.) (Registered New York Breds allowed 3 lbs.)

Value of Race: $32,500 Winner $19,500; second $6,500; third $3,575; fourth $1,950; fifth $975. Mutuel Pool $540,399.00 Exacta Pool $501,638.00 Trifecta Pool $397,300.00 Superfecta Pool $164,386.00

Last Raced	Horse	M/Eqt.	A.	Wt	PP	St	¼	½	¾	Str	Fin	Jockey	Cl'g Pr	Odds $1
23Nov02 ^{2}Aqu^{2}	Gail's Drive	Lf	4	116	2	4	6$^{1\frac{1}{2}}$	3$^{\frac{1}{2}}$	3^{1}	2^{1}	1^{nk}	Luzzi M J	30000	2.35
7Nov02 ^{9}Aqu^{2}	Borntoberegal	Lf	5	120	4	2	2^{1}	2$^{\frac{1}{2}}$	2^{1}	1^{1}	2$^{5\frac{1}{4}}$	Migliore R	35000	*2.35
24Nov02 ^{5}Aqu^{8}	Hourly Storm	L	4	120	5	1	1$^{\frac{1}{2}}$	1^{1}	1^{hd}	3^{3}	3$^{1\frac{1}{4}}$	Mojica R Jr	35000	14.60
24Nov02 ^{5}Aqu^{7}	Bedroom Kisser	Lbf	4	115	8	8	7^{1}	8^{5}	6$^{\frac{1}{2}}$	5^{1}	4$^{\frac{3}{4}}$	McKee J^{5}	35000	8.80
15Nov02 ^{7}Aqu^{4}	Fighten Beezie	Lf	6	115	6	3	3$^{\frac{1}{2}}$	6^{1}	5^{3}	4^{hd}	5$^{1\frac{3}{4}}$	Chavez Luis^{5}	35000	20.70
23Nov02 ^{2}Aqu^{4}	Gunning	Lb	7	113	9	5	5^{hd}	4^{hd}	4^{1}	6^{6}	6$^{10\frac{1}{4}}$	Persaud R	30000	7.90
1Nov02 ^{5}Aqu^{1}	Best Shot Yet	L	6	119	10	9	8$^{1\frac{1}{2}}$	7$^{1\frac{1}{2}}$	7^{1}	7^{4}	7$^{3\frac{1}{4}}$	Arroyo N Jr	35000	14.40
29Nov02 ^{10}Aqu^{4}	Bianco Appeal	L	4	116	7	10	10	10	9^{2}	8^{1}	8$^{1\frac{1}{2}}$	Carlos M	30000	41.25
7Feb02 ^{7}GP^{6}	You Know Who	Lbf	4	120	3	6	4^{hd}	5$^{\frac{1}{2}}$	8^{2}	9^{3}	9$^{4\frac{1}{4}}$	Velazquez J R	35000	9.90
11Nov02 ^{3}Aqu^{8}	Winter Glitter	Lb	5	122	1	7	9^{3}	9^{3}	10	10	10	Toscano P R	35000	13.90

***—Actual Betting Favorite.**

OFF AT 4:13 Start Good. Won driving. Track muddy.
TIME :24^{3}, :49^{1}, 1:14^{1}, 1:39^{3}, 1:46^{1} (:24.79, :49.37, 1:14.25, 1:39.63, 1:46.21)

$2 Mutuel Prices:

2–GAIL'S DRIVE	6.70	3.60	2.90
4–BORNTOBEREGAL		3.50	2.80
5–HOURLY STORM			4.90

$2 EXACTA 2–4 PAID $18.00 $2 TRIFECTA 2–4–5 PAID $99.50 $2 SUPERFECTA 2–4–5–9 PAID $850.00

B. g, by Ide–Gail's Brush, by Broad Brush. Trainer Levine Bruce N. Bred by Willmott Stable (Ky).

GAIL'S DRIVE was rated on the inside, came off the rail approaching the stretch, split rivals passing the furlong marker and then rallied inside of BORNTOBEREGAL to prevail late. BORNTOBEREGAL tracked the pace on the outside, made his bid nearing the quarter pole, took over and fought gamely to the wire. HOURLY STORM set the pace and weakened in the stretch. BEDROOM KISSER closed belatedly. FIGHTEN BEEZIE raced between rivals and had no rally. GUNNING chased and tired. BEST SHOT YET raced five wide on the clubhouse turn and tired. BIANCO APPEAL did not factor. YOU KNOW WHO raced between rivals and faded. WINTER GLITTER did not factor.

Owners— 1, Baron Robert J; 2, Boyan Thomas C & Learn Jr; 3, Nunn David; 4, Franks John; 5, Piazza Giuseppina & One Pond Stable; 6, Calabrese Anthony; 7, Fried Albert Jr; 8, Gerson Brad; 9, Scatuorchio James T; 10, Morgan Brian P

Trainers—1, Levine Bruce N; 2, Hushion Michael E; 3, Nunn David; 4, Martin Gregory F; 5, Sciacca Gary; 6, Lalman Dennis; 7, Schosberg Richard; 8, Pantaleo Joseph; 9, Pletcher Todd A; 10, Orseno Joseph

Borntoberegal was claimed by Kupferberg Saul; trainer, Parisella John.

Scratched— Alter Ego (6Dec02 ^{9}AQU^{1}), Personal Journey (23Nov02 ^{2}AQU^{6}), Makem Hagar (28Oct02 ^{8}DEL^{3})

$2 Daily Double (9–2) Paid $23.40; Daily Double Pool $285,851.
$2 Pick Three (4–9–2) Paid $117.00; Pick Three Pool $146,696.
$2 Pick Four (3–4–9–2) Paid $348.50; Pick Four Pool $233,501.

Aqueduct Attendance: 9,557 Mutuel Pool: $1,118,388.00 ITW Mutuel Pool: $3,210,138.00 ISW Mutuel Pool: $7,237,280.00

FIFTH RACE
Aqueduct
DECEMBER 14, 2002

1 MILE 70 YARDS. (Inner Dirt) (1.384) MAIDEN SPECIAL WEIGHT. Purse $42,000. (Up To $8,245 NYSBFOA) For Maiden Fillies Two Years Old. Weight 120 lbs. (Registered New York Breds allowed 3 lbs.).

Value of Race: $42,000 Winner $25,200; second $8,400; third $4,620; fourth $2,520; fifth $1,260. Mutuel Pool $455,958.00 Exacta Pool $442,981.00 Trifecta Pool $331,169.00

Last Raced	Horse	M/Eqt.A.Wt	PP	St	1/4	1/2	3/4	Str	Fin	Jockey	Odds $1
20Nov02 2CD2	Show Bug	Lf 2 120	2	8	4hd	41	42	3½	1nk	Luzzi M J	5.20
14Nov02 5Aqu2	Arctic Rose	L 2 120	1	1	21½	21	2½	1½	23½	Carr D	1.55
23Nov02 4Aqu2	Three Roses	L 2 115	4	4	11	1½	1hd	21	3½	McKee J5	4.20
24Nov02 1Aqu2	Quiet Julia	L 2 120	3	2	3½	3hd	32	45	44	Smith A E	9.80
15Nov02 3Aqu4	April Eyes	Lb 2 120	6	3	73	74	52	52	53	Gryder A T	13.90
	Day's Sunset	L 2 120	9	10	83	85	88	7½	61	Samyn J L	11.60
17Nov02 3Aqu3	Lucy Angelicus	Lf 2 120	10	7	6½	6hd	7½	6hd	7¾	Lopez C C	9.00
17Nov02 5Aqu5	Royal Sweep	Lb 2 115	5	5	52	5hd	61	812	818½	Chavez Luis5	41.00
14Nov02 5Aqu6	Lucky Lady Liz	2 120	8	6	910	910	95	95	911½	Castellano J J	29.25
	Blue Lagoon	2 120	7	9	10	10	10	10	10	Arroyo N Jr	33.00

OFF AT 2:24 Start Good. Won driving. Track sloppy.

TIME :23², :48, 1:13⁴, 1:41¹, 1:45⁴ (:23.46, :48.03, 1:13.96, 1:41.35, 1:45.88)

$2 Mutuel Prices:

2 – SHOW BUG	12.40	5.20	3.70
1 – ARCTIC ROSE		3.40	2.70
4 – THREE ROSES			3.10

$2 EXACTA 2–1 PAID $33.20 $2 TRIFECTA 2–1–4 PAID $98.50

B. f, (Apr), by Holy Bull–Zulu Dance, by Danzador. Trainer Levine Bruce N. Bred by John T L Jones Jr (Ky).

SHOW BUG was well placed on the inside, responded when roused in upper stretch, rallied inside of ARTICE ROSE in the two path and prevailed in the final strides. ARCTIC ROSE raced firmly in hand while two wide on the first turn, settled into stride stalking the leader, challenged between rivals on the far turn, then edged clear and battled gamely to the wire. THREE ROSES set the pace on the inside and tired in the stretch. QUIET JULIA stalked the pace while three wide, bid for the lead at the quarter pole and then flattened out. APRIL EYES raced inside and had no rally. DAY'S SUNSET failed to threaten. LUCY ANGELICUS raced between rivals and tired. ROYAL SWEEP raced three wide and faded. LUCKY LADY LIZ was outrun. BLUE LAGOON raced far back throughout.

Owners— 1, Valente Roddy J; 2, Silverleaf Farms Inc; 3, Buckram Oak Farm; 4, Bourke Kieran Terranova Thomas & O'; 5, Jester Michael W; 6, Phillips Joan G & John W; 7, Hackman William M; 8, Farmer Tracy; 9, Coppola Albert P, 10, Overbrook Farm

Trainers—1, Levine Bruce N; 2, Kimmel John C; 3, Zito Nicholas P; 4, Nevin Michael; 5, Schettino Dominick A; 6, Toner James J; 7, Thompson J Willard; 8, McPeek Kenneth G; 9, Donk David; 10, Lukas D Wayne

Scratched— Unbridled Valor (15Nov02 3AQU2), Urania (29Nov02 3AQU9), Indy Five Hundred (1Dec02 6AQU3), Freei (1Dec02 6AQU4)

$2 Pick Three (2-5-2) Paid $675.00; Pick Three Pool $81,113.

16

CLOSING NOTES

MY BASIC PHILOSOPHY on Thoroughbred handicapping can be summed up as follows: In order to be successful in this game, you must have an edge!

Whether it is early speed, closing kick, class, current condition, or even as simple an angle as a proven mud-runner's loving today's wet surface, wherever an edge exists, it must be taken advantage of if one is to be successful.

In mathematics, two plus two is always four. In Thoroughbred handicapping, that's not always the case. If a certain angle works today, there are no guarantees it will work tomorrow. The main reason is that the set of circumstances that surrounds each race is always different. The factors that make up the inconsistent racing equation are never the same.

I have always felt strongly that the most basic concept to successful handicapping came down to finding a method that you believe in and is right for you, along with performance angles that work on a highly consistent basis. If these methods and angles are successful, they will identify outstanding edges in many different areas within a race. The next step would be to consider all the added racing information gathered from your race-result charts. Then the final step would be to invest wisely and strategically in these discovered edges.

The best way to stay successful in this game is to keep striving to learn new angles, theories, and methods. Few things in racing stay the same for very long, and all the variables are constantly changing.

I was taught at a very young age to identify angles and realize the value of racing principles. One of the more important things my father taught me about handicapping is how to identify performance angles and training angles that can indicate when a horse is about to run a big race. I learned that within most racing scenarios, it's not the fastest or the best horse that usually wins a given race, but the one that can benefit the most from the clash of running styles within today's field.

If you can solve the puzzle of why a given horse won a particular race, then the odds are in your favor that you might be able to detect this same angle or edge the next time you handicap. This is why my father instructed me to go through each race on a card and try and find out what the winning horse was showing in his past performances. Years later, I have come to realize that such investigative thinking helped me learn many important racing principles.

This method of handicapping can truly elevate your game. I believe that a handsome profit from the races awaits all those willing to put some time and effort into charting races.

ABOUT THE AUTHOR

Sheryl Borg

NICK BORG HAS been part of the quality-assurance team of *Daily Racing Form* since 1992. He is the author of three handicapping books: *Ultimate Pace Handicapping* (1995), *The Hidden Par Method* (1998), and *Win-Generate 2000* (1999). He also contributed a chapter on pace analysis for DRF Press's *A Difference of Opinion* (1998).

Since 1995, he has been the "Angle of the Month" columnist for *American Turf Monthly* as well as a weekly columnist for *Las Vegas Sports News*.